CHOICES

PRE-INTERMEDIATE WORKBOOK

with Audio CD

T0345705

SUE KAY • VAUGHAN JONES

WITH ONLINE SKILLS BY GAVIN DUDENEY AND NICKY HOCKLY

CONTENTS

TOPIC TALK – VOCABULARY

1 Complete the table with *at, in* or *on*.

on	___	___
Wednesday	7 a.m.	the morning
Sunday	the weekend	the afternoon
morning		

2 Add more time expressions to the correct column in Exercise 1.

Monday   four-thirty   night   the evening
Saturday afternoon   18.00   Thursday night
August   2010   14 February

3 Complete each sentence with the correct preposition.

1 __On__ Mondays, I always feel tired.
2 _____ the weekend, I go shopping.
3 _____ Friday night, I go swimming.
4 _____ August, I go on holiday.
5 _____ 31 December, I usually go to a party.
6 _____ the evening, I do my homework.

4 Choose the correct verb.

1 What time do you *go/sleep* to bed at the weekend?
2 Where do you usually *do/make* your homework?
3 Do you *do/have* lunch at school?
4 Do you *go on/play* computer games?
5 When do you *spend/do* time with your family?
6 Do you *have/feel* tired at the end of the week?

5 Complete the sentences with the correct words.

1 Students at my school can do __extra__ __classes__ of maths and English to help them.
2 I _____ jogging on Wednesdays.
3 I _____ jobs in the house _____ the weekend.
4 When I _____ tired I _____ time at home with my family.
5 I _____ at 7.30 on Saturdays because I _____ basketball in a team.

6 Complete the text.

do   feel   go   go on   go to   ~~have~~
play (x 2)   sleep   spend

In the morning I get up late and I don't ¹ __have__ a shower. I don't walk to school – I get the bus. At home, I never ² _____ any homework. I ³ _____ messenger and chat to my friends, or I ⁴ _____ computer games. At the weekend I never ⁵ _____ swimming or ⁶ _____ football. I ⁷ _____ time on the internet. I don't ⁸ _____ parties. I ⁹ _____ twelve hours a night but I always ¹⁰ _____ tired.

7 Use all the verbs and phrases below to write a short text about yourself.

do   get up   go to   hours a night
play   spend time with

_____
_____
_____
_____
_____
_____
_____

① Read the text and choose the best ending to the sentences.

1 Natalie is living **a** at home. **b** with the circus.
2 At the weekend, she **a** works. **b** goes out with friends.
3 She does **a** one performance a week. **b** six performances a week.
4 Circus people **a** have dinner together. **b** don't have dinner together.
5 Natalie goes swimming **a** because it's good for her body. **b** for fun.

Word Builder Making adjectives

② Make adjectives from the nouns. Check your answers in the text.

1 wonder ___wonderful___
2 friend _____
3 craze _____
4 hard work _____
5 profession _____
6 success _____
7 danger _____
8 help _____
9 fame _____

NATALIE IS TRAINING TO BE A TRAPEZE ARTIST. HERE, SHE TALKS TO US ABOUT LIFE WITH THE CIRCUS.

'I love living with the circus. I have a lot of fun, but I also work really hard. I work long hours and I don't have any free time at the weekend. I only have one day off a week when I can go out with my friends.

The day begins very early for the circus. I'm not a morning person – I hate getting up early. But I need to practise a lot because I'm still training. So, on a typical day, I get up at 6 a.m. and go jogging before breakfast. I practise for about eight hours every day, and then we do a show in the evening.

At midday, everybody eats together. It's really important to eat a big lunch because we don't have time to have dinner. After a show, I have a snack and go to bed, but I often can't sleep so I listen to music or read to relax.

On my day off, I often sleep all day. Sometimes I go to town with my circus friends and we go shopping, sit in cafés or go to the cinema.

I travel a lot with the circus. Every two weeks we move to a different city. I never sleep more than three nights in the same town. Sometimes I wake up and can't remember where we are! I miss my family and friends, but I never get lonely because I have a circus family now. The circus is full of wonderful characters. Circus people are really friendly, and a bit crazy, but they're hard-working and professional, too.

I want to be successful, but the job of trapeze artist is dangerous and bad for my body. I go swimming or do yoga as often as I can, and that's helpful.

The best thing is when I'm on the trapeze – I love seeing people's faces. One day, I hope to be a famous trapeze artist.'

3 Complete the sentences with the correct adjectives from Exercise 2.

1 According to Natalie, circus people are _friendly_, a little _____ but _____.
2 A trapeze artist's job is _____ but _____.
3 Natalie wants to be _____ and _____.

Sentence Builder Linkers

4 Complete the sentences with the words below.

and   and then (x 2)   but   or (x 2)

1 Natalie gets up early, goes for a run _and then_ she has breakfast.
2 On a typical day, Natalie has breakfast, lunch _____ a snack in the evening.
3 She misses her real family _____ she never gets lonely.
4 After a show, she has a snack _____ she reads _____ listens to music.
5 She goes swimming _____ does yoga because it's good for her body.

5 Use the linkers in brackets to join the sentences.

1 At the weekend, I sleep until 10 a.m. I go out with friends. (and then)
   At the weekend, I sleep until 10 a.m. and then I
   go out with friends.
2 After school I sometimes play football. I sometimes play basketball. (or)
   _____
3 I feel tired at night. I always do my homework. (but)
   _____
4 On Saturdays I spend time with my friends. I do jobs in the house. (and)
   _____
5 What do you prefer – jogging? Do you prefer swimming? (or)
   _____

Writing

6 Choose a person in your family. Write about their day. Use adjectives and linkers.

My brother is a student, on a typical day he ...
_____
_____
_____
_____
_____
_____
_____
_____

Present Simple and Continuous

REMEMBER

Complete exercises A–D before you start this lesson.

A **Write positive or negative sentences with the Present Simple.**

1 I get up before 7 a.m. _I don't get up before 7 a.m._
2 I don't enjoy exams. _____
3 My father does jobs in the house.
   _____
4 I don't have lunch at school. _____
5 My mother watches football on TV.
   _____
6 My friends don't eat fast food.
   _____

B **Make Present Simple questions.**

1 you / play basketball? _Do you play basketball?_
2 you / go to extra maths classes?
   _____
3 your friends / enjoy English? _____
4 your teacher / smoke? _____
5 you / sleep more than eight hours a night?
   _____
6 your city / have a good football team?
   _____

C **Complete the sentences using the Present Continuous.**

1 I usually go to school by car but today (I / walk)
   I'm walking .
2 I don't read much but (I / read) _____ a great book at the moment.
3 (Mum / not / work) _____ today, she's shopping.
4 My brother isn't very good at French so (he / have) _____ extra classes this year.
5 My friends and I usually play basketball on Saturday but (we / not play) _____ today because we've got a lot of homework to do.

D **Order the words in the sentences.**

1 wearing / you / are / what? _What are you wearing?_
2 are / sitting / where / you? _____
3 using / you / a pen or a pencil / are?
   _____
4 doing / is / everybody in your family / what / at the moment? _____

❶ * **Look at the picture on page 7. Complete the sentences with the Present Simple or the Present Continuous form of the words in brackets.**

1 Ben's _studying_ for his exams. (study)
2 He sometimes _____ tennis but he _____ at the moment. (play)
3 He _____ a Harry Potter book. He _____ every day. (read)
4 He _____ to his girlfriend. (talk)
5 He _____ on his bed. (lie)
6 He _____ U2. His brother _____ U2 – he thinks they are boring. (love)

❷ ** **Make questions with the Present Simple or Present Continuous.**

1 you / listen / to the news?
   No, I'm listening to music.
   Are you listening to the news?
2 it / snow in your city?
   Sometimes but not every year.
   _____?
3 you / text / one of your friends?
   No, I'm looking at the photos on my phone.
   _____?
4 you / use an English-English dictionary?
   No, I prefer a bilingual one.
   _____?
5 your father / cook?
   No, I don't think so. Maybe mum is.
   _____?
6 you / wear / new shoes?
   No, these are at least two years old.
   _____?
7 where / she / come from?
   She comes from Spain.
   _____?
8 what / she / wear today?
   She's wearing jeans.
   _____?
9 what time / he / usually get up?
   At seven o'clock.
   _____?

3 *** Complete the text with the correct form of the verbs below.

cook go have not like ~~live~~ read run
stay swim train not train watch

I ¹ _live_ in an apartment in London, but at the moment I ² _____ with a friend in the country. We ³ _____ for a triathlon. Every morning we ⁴ _____ for a two-hour cycle. Then we ⁵ _____ lunch. My friend ⁶ _____ really healthy food – meat, fish, eggs and vegetables – but unfortunately he ⁷ _____ pasta – and it's my favourite. In the afternoon, we ⁸ _____ fifteen kilometres and in the evening we ⁹ _____ in the river. On Sundays we ¹⁰ _____ – that's today! So my friend ¹¹ _____ the newspaper and I ¹² _____ a triathlon on the TV.

Grammar Alive Talking on your mobile

4 ** Use the cues to write three mobile conversations.

A: *Hi, Jack. Where are you? Can you talk now?*
B: *I'm on the other line. I'm talking to my mum. Can I call you back?*
A: *Okay. Speak to you in a bit.*

- on the other line / talk to my mum
- cinema / wait for film to start
- Post Office / buy some stamps
- bicycle / go into town

Grammar Alive Talking about habits

5 ** Use the cues to make questions and answers.

1 **A:** have lunch at school?
  B: ✗ - wait until I get home
  A: *Do you have lunch at school?*
  B: *No, I don't. I wait until I get home.*

2 **A:** do any sports?
  B: ✔ - play football and basketball
  A: _____
  B: _____

3 **A:** go to any extra classes?
  B: ✗ - but do a lot of homework every night
  A: _____
  B: _____

4 **A:** go to parties?
  B: ✔ - but never dance
  A: _____
  B: _____

5 **A:** do / any jobs in the house
  B: ✔ - but my brother not / do anything.
  A: _____
  B: _____

SKILLS
Listening

1 Label the picture.

1 _helmet_
2 _____
3 _____
4 _____
5 _____
6 _____

2 Complete the text with the words below.

background because behind ~~can~~ definitely
perhaps probably

In the foreground you ¹___can___ see two people. They're ²_____ in a café because you can see the waiter in the ³_____. Matt is sitting down and he's looking at his laptop. ⁴_____ he's a cyclist ⁵_____ there's a cycle helmet on the table. Lucy is standing ⁶_____ Matt. She's holding a bottle of water. Lucy and Matt are ⁷_____ friends because she's looking at his laptop.

3 **1.2** Listen to David and Sally discussing holiday photos of Sally's travels around Europe. Which two photos do they mention?

Check Your Progress 1

1 Routines **Complete the description.**

At the weekend I do lots of sport. On Saturday morning, I get up and ¹_____ swimming. After that I ²_____ breakfast and then I ³_____ my homework. In the afternoon I ⁴_____ football. On Sundays, I ⁵_____ cycling. After that my friends usually call for me and we ⁶_____ to the park and play basketball. In the evening, I watch TV or ⁷_____ Messenger. I go to bed early because I'm really tired!

/7

2 Making adjectives **Complete the sentences with the correct form of the words in brackets.**

1 I don't like extreme sports – I'm not very _____ (adventure).
2 Many _____ (fame) actors live in Beverley Hills.
3 Everyone in the village is very _____ (friend) to us.
4 The teacher made some _____ (help) comments.
5 We went to the circus yesterday. It was _____ (wonder).
6 My friends are great, and a bit _____ (craze).

/6

3 Races **Complete the sentences with the correct words.**

1 My brother is training for a triathlon. He's really good at running and cycling, but he isn't very good at _____.
2 I'm going on a cycling holiday to Morocco. It's going to be very sunny so I need a good pair of _____.
3 I love open water events but I hate cold water. I always wear a _____ to keep me warm.
4 My friend is training for a _____. She has to run more than forty-two kilometres. I couldn't do it.
5 It's important to take a water _____ when you go cycling.
6 I always wear _____ when I ski to protect my eyes.
7 It's important to wear a _____ when you go cycling.

/7

4 Present Simple and Present Continuous **Complete the dialogue with the Present Simple or the Present Continuous form of the words in brackets.**

Mrs Jones: Hello Emma. What are you doing here? ¹_____ (I/not often see) you in the supermarket.

Emma: Oh, hello Mrs Jones. No, ²_____ (mum/usually do) the shopping, but ³_____ (she/spend) the day with a friend today.

Mrs Jones: Oh, that's nice. What ⁴_____ (you/buy)? Ah, lots of vegetables.

Emma: ⁵_____ (I/prefer) ready-made meals, but ⁶_____ (my mum/think) I need to eat more fruit and vegetables.

Mrs Jones: She's right! ⁷_____ _____ (I/not/eat) ready-made meals and ⁸_____ (I/have) lots of energy. ⁹_____ (I/be) seventy, you know!

Emma: That's great Mrs Jones. Nice to see you. Bye!

/9

5 Describing photos **Look at the photo of Paris on page 8 and complete the text with the correct words.**

The photo shows a typical scene in Paris. It's ¹_____ very hot because the people are wearing summer clothes. In the ²_____ of the photo we can see a boat. In the ³_____ a couple are having coffee. On the ⁴_____ there is a girl on her mobile. On the ⁵_____ left there is a man reading the newspaper. We know the photo is in Paris because in the ⁶_____ you can just see the Eiffel Tower.

/6

TOTAL SCORE */35*

Module Diary

1 Look at the objectives on page 5 in the Students' Book. Choose three and evaluate your learning.

1 Now I can _____
   well / quite well / with problems.
2 Now I can _____
   well / quite well / with problems.
3 Now I can _____
   well / quite well / with problems.

2 Look at your results. What language areas in this module do you need to study more?

Sound Choice 1

1 **1.4** Grammar – 3rd person endings **Listen to the chants. Match the ending sound /s/, /z/ or /iz/ to the correct column. Then practise the chants.**

/s/		
She works.	She jogs.	She teaches.
He sleeps.	He swims.	He boxes.
She thinks.	She skis.	She dances.
He eats.	He wins.	He watches.

2 **1.5** Grammar – 3rd person endings **Put the verbs in the correct column and then listen, check and repeat.**

choose cook eat feel go guess match play spend take taste use

/s/	/z/	/iz/
cooks		

3 **1.6** Consonants – /w/ and /h/ **Complete the tongue twisters with Who, Why, How or Which. Then listen, check and repeat.**

1 _Why_ worry when we're winning?
2 _____ watch works well under water?
3 _____ hard is Mr Hall's history homework?
4 _____ had her holiday in a horrible hotel?

4 **1.7** Vowels and spelling – /ɒ/, /ɔː/ and /əʊ/ **Listen and repeat the words. Underline the word with a different vowel sound in each group.**

1 what / job / clock / watch / s<u>aw</u>
2 sport / boat / walk / floor / ball
3 roast / slow / coat / want / note

5 Vowels and spelling – /ɒ/, /ɜː/ and /əʊ/ **Match the words from Exercise 4 to the correct vowel sound.**

1 /ɒ/ what, _____, _____, _____, _____ + _____

2 /ɔː/ sport, _____, _____, _____, _____ + _____

3 /əʊ/ roast _____, _____, _____, _____ + _____

6 **1.8** Difficult words – word stress **Two syllables or three? Write the number of syllables and mark the stress. Then listen, check and repeat.**

1 alóne _____2_____
2 beautiful _____
3 breakfast _____
4 different _____
5 eccentric _____
6 historic _____
7 recipe _____
8 relaxed _____
9 routine _____
10 shower _____
11 successful _____
12 vegetable _____

10

TOPIC TALK – VOCABULARY

1 Put the words into the correct category (a-d) in the network.

air guitar   chess   ~~coins~~   gymnastics   jewellery
model aeroplanes   photography   the piano   sports   stamps

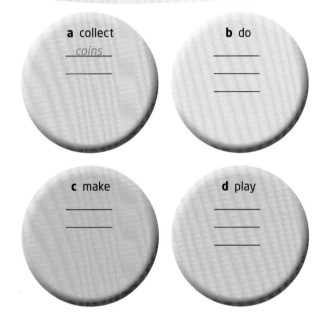

a collect
coins
_____

b do
_____
_____

c make
_____
_____

d play
_____
_____

2 Match phrases (1-6) with phrases (a-f) to make sentences.

1 I'm really _c_
2 I play tennis every ___
3 I like ___
4 I don't ___
5 I'd like ___
6 I like playing ___

a weekend.
b to try surfing.
c into playing computer games.
d enjoy singing.
e air guitar.
f collecting music DVDs.

3 Complete the sentences with one word.

1 I don't enjoy _doing_ sport.
2 I like _____ model aeroplanes.
3 I'm really _____ acting.
4 I'd like _____ try free running.
5 I don't _____ stamps.
6 I don't like _____ board games.
7 I play football _____ weekend.

4 Underline the negative adjective in each group of words.

1 cool <u>boring</u> relaxing
2 silly creative exciting
3 challenging dangerous fun
4 healthy interesting difficult

5 Order the words in the sentences.

1 acting / because / challenging / I / it's / love
   _____ *I love acting because it's challenging.* _____
2 because / dancing / fun / I / it's / like
   _____
3 because / boring / chess / don't / I / it's / like / playing
   _____
4 air guitar / playing / because / don't / enjoy / I / it's / silly
   _____
5 because / creative / enjoy / I / it's / jewellery / making
   _____
6 because / cool / free running / I'd / it's / like / to / try
   _____

6 Complete the dialogue with the words below.

~~at~~   because   doing   every   going   hobby
into   like   the   to

A: What are you doing ¹__*at*__ the weekend?
B: I'm ²_____ cycling. I do it ³_____ weekend with two friends from school. Why don't you come with us?
A: Oh, no thanks, I don't enjoy ⁴_____ sport!
B: What do you ⁵_____ doing in your free time?
A: I'm really ⁶_____ photography. I like it ⁷_____ it's creative.
B: I'd like ⁸_____ try photography, but I'm not very creative and I don't have a good camera.
A: It's an expensive ⁹_____ but it's fun. I also like playing ¹⁰_____ piano. I like doing relaxing things in my free time.

REMEMBER

Complete exercise A before you start this lesson.

A Complete the sentences with the Present Perfect form of the words in brackets.

1 I *'ve never eaten* in a McDonald's restaurant. (never eat)
2 I _____ all my homework. (do)
3 My mother _____ to Scotland. (go)
4 My brother and I _____ the *Tour de France*. (not see)
5 My friends _____ my parents. (not meet)

Complete exercises B-E before you start lesson 6.

B Look at the nouns. Are they countable or uncountable. Write *a*, *an* or nothing (-).

1 ___*an*___ apple   6 _____ money
2 _____ bus   7 _____ orange
3 _____ egg   8 _____ party
4 _____ furniture   9 _____ pasta
5 _____ information 10 _____ rice

C Write plural nouns for each countable noun in Exercise B.

1 an apple → *apples*
_____
_____
_____
_____
_____

D Underline the correct word.

1 I have *a/some* homework to do this evening.
2 I have *a/some* new mobile phone.
3 I have *a/some* pop music on my MP3 player.
4 I have *a/some* money in my pocket.
5 I have *an/some* old bicycle.

E Make the sentences in Exercise D negative with *a/an* or *any*.

1 *I don't have any homework to do this evening.*
2 _____
3 _____
4 _____
5 _____

❶ * Match the sentence beginnings (1-6) with the sentence endings (a-e).

1 Emma's upset, _*d*_   a he's finished his exams.
2 Dave's very happy, ___   b I've made a big salad.
3 Tim looks tired, ___   c she's gone out.
4 Beth isn't here, ___   d she's lost her MP3 player.
5 That family don't live   e he hasn't slept very well.
  here, ___   f they've moved.
6 Lunch is ready, ___

❷ ** Look at the pictures and use the cues to write sentences.

1 He / fall / love
   He's fallen in love.

2 He / lose / keys
   _____

3 She / buy / new dress
   _____

4 They / sell / house
   _____

③ ** Complete the sentences with the verbs in brackets in the Present Perfect.

1 **A:** Pauline (lose) __has lost__ her phone
  B: She (hasn't lost) __hasn't lost__ her phone. It's in her bag. I can hear it.

2 **A:** (you / forget) _____ that it's my birthday today?
  B: Er ... no. I (not forget). _____. I've ... er ... got a surprise for you. You can have it ... er ... later.

3 **A:** You look happy. (you / win) _____ some money?
  B: (no, / not) _____ but I (pass) _____ my English exam.

4 **A:** I (write) _____ ten pages of work on the computer and now I can't find it.
  B: Don't worry. I can find it for you.
  A: You're very clever.
  B: No, but I (make) _____ the same mistake many times.

5 **A:** What's wrong?
  B: I (eat) _____ some food but the 'eat before' date is March 22. It's March 25 today.
  A: That's okay. I (read) _____ about 'eat before' dates. Three days isn't too bad.

6 **A:** You (not clean) _____ the kitchen. Look at this mess.
  B: I'm sorry but I (make) _____ you a cake
  A: Half a cake.
  B: Oh yes. I (eat) _____ some. It's very nice.

④ *** Complete the dialogue with the Present Perfect form of the words below.

> buy   do   lose   meet   ~~start~~

Ann: Hi Rose. How are you?
Rose: I feel really relaxed because [1]I_'ve started_ my holidays.
Ann: You look fantastic. [2]_____ you _____ something to your hair?
Rose: No, I haven't. But [3]I _____ five kilos. My brother wants to get fit so he [4]_____ a new bicycle and we go cycling together every day.
Ann: How is your brother?
Rose: He's very happy. [5]He _____ a lovely girl.

Grammar Alive Explaining causes

⑤ ** Use the cues to write dialogues.

1 **A:** I / angry
  B: you / lose something?
  A: No / I / have an argument with my sister
  A: _I'm angry._
  B: _Have you lost something?_
  A: _No, I've had an argument with my sister._

2 **A:** I / excited
  B: you / win something?
  A: No / I / pass my driving test
  A: _____
  B: _____
  A: _____

3 **A:** I / worried
  B: you / forgot something?
  A: No / I / not receive my new passport
  A: _____
  B: _____
  A: _____

4 **A:** I / very happy
  B: you / meet somebody new?
  A: No / I / win a competition
  A: _____
  B: _____
  A: _____

5 **A:** I / tired
  B: you / run all the way to your house?
  A: No / I / swim 1000 metres in the swimming pool
  A: _____
  B: _____
  A: _____

6 **A:** I / sad
  B: you / fail your maths test?
  A: No / I / lose my mobile phone
  A: _____
  B: _____
  A: _____

① 🔊 **1.9** **Listen to a conversation between two friends, Claire and Rob. Choose the correct answers.**

1 What is Claire worried about?
   a She can't play computer games.
   b She hasn't got a birthday present for her brother.
   c It's her birthday tomorrow.

2 What sort of computer games does Claire's brother like?
   a role-playing games
   b simulation games
   c She doesn't know.

3 What does Rob think of Dragon Quest?
   a The graphics are amazing.
   b It's brilliant.
   c It's really old.

4 What does Claire's brother enjoy doing in his free time?
   a playing computer games
   b playing guitar
   c playing football

5 What does Claire think of the football game?
   a It's exciting.
   b It's silly.
   c It's different.

6 What does Claire decide to get her brother for his birthday?
   a a football computer game
   b a football shirt
   c a football

Sentence Builder Opinions

② 🔊 **1.9** **Are the sentences true (T) or false (F)? Listen to the conversation again and check your answers.**

1 Rob doesn't know about computer games. ___
2 Claire doesn't think role-playing games are very interesting. ___
3 Rob thinks the graphics on Final Fantasy are amazing. ___
4 Rob thinks *Music Maker Rockstar* is a silly game. ___
5 Rob thinks computer football games are better than real games. ___
6 Claire doesn't think computer football games are very expensive. ___

Word Builder Modifiers

③ **Choose the correct words to complete the dialogue.**

A: What games do you have on your phone?
B: I've got loads: *Angry Birds* is ¹ _quite_ good. *(quite/absolutely)*
A: *Angry Birds*? That's ² _____ silly isn't it? *(absolutely/a bit)*
B: I know, but I love it. I've got *Chess Quest* too and that's ³ _____ fantastic *(very/absolutely)*.
A: Chess is too difficult for me. I like games with ⁴ _____ great graphics, like *Red Nova*. *(really/a bit)*
B: I don't know that one.
A: Oh, it's ⁵ _____ amazing. It came out a few years ago, but it's still the best. *(very/really)*
B: I sometimes play *SimCity*, but it's ⁶ _____ long. *(very/absolutely)*

GRAMMAR

some, any, no, a lot of, a few, a little

Complete exercises B-E on page 12 before you start this lesson.

1 * Put the nouns in the correct column.

~~athletics~~ euro fiesta food fun money music restaurant ~~runner~~ song time tourist travel watch

UNCOUNTABLE	COUNTABLE
athletics	*a runner*

2 ** Complete the sentences with *some* or *any*.

1 Are there ___*any*___ good clothes shops in your city?

2 Let's go out and have _____ fun.

3 Have you got _____ cola in the fridge?

4 I want to buy _____ new trainers.

5 I never have _____ luck with the lottery.

6 There aren't _____ pens that work in this house!

3 * Write six sentences using the words and phrases from boxes A, B and C.

A	B	C
I have I don't have	a few a little a lot of any no some	friends. money.

I have a few friends.

_____

_____

_____

_____

_____

4 *** Complete the dialogue with the words below. You can use each word more than once.

any   few (x 2)   little   lot (x 3)   no (x 2)   some

BRAZIL

Rio de Janeiro

A: Can I ask you a ¹___*few*___ questions about festivals in Brazil?

B: Sure! There are a ²_____ of festivals in Brazil but I think the Rio carnival is the best!

A: Really? Why?

B: Well, the highlight of the carnival is the costumes. A ³_____ of people wear amazing clothes. At the Rio carnival, people just want to dance and have ⁴_____ fun.

A: When and where is the carnival?

B: The carnival is forty days before Easter and lasts for a ⁵_____ days. There's a ⁶_____ of noise, so people only get a ⁷_____ sleep during the carnival.

A: Are there ⁸_____ other activities?

B: Yes there are. For example, street parties and bands.

A: Do you go to the Rio carnival every year?

B: Yes, but it's very crowded now. There are ⁹_____ hotel rooms left in February and ¹⁰_____ seats on the trains but it doesn't matter. I always come. I think it's amazing.

Workshop 1

Writing

1 Read the letter. Match the parts of the letter (1–5) with the sections (a–e).

1 Who do you have to contact? _e_
2 When and where is the party? ___
3 What is the party for? ___
4 How much are the tickets? ___
5 What music is there? ___

SUMMER HOLIDAY PARTY

a
We're organising a party to celebrate the summer holidays.

In the School Sports Hall:
8 p.m. on Saturday 29 June. b

c **Live band and disco.**

d **Fancy dress competition**

Tickets: £5 Soft drinks and food provided.

Contact Elana on 0987 352 67 e

2 Answer the questions in Exercise 1.

Sentence Builder Purpose linkers

3 Choose the correct words to complete the sentences.

1 They've invited me to a party *to/for* Lara's birthday.
2 They're having a party *to/for* celebrate the end of term.
3 Somebody has organised a football match *for/to* raise money for sports equipment.
4 We want to buy a present *for/to* Ben's birthday.
5 I'm going to town *for/to* buy some new party clothes.

4 Write an invitation for a birthday party, an end of exams party or a New Year's Eve party. Use the invitation above to help you.

Speaking

1 🔊1.10 Complete the dialogue with the correct form of the verbs below. Listen again and check.

> because   like   ~~Maybe~~   in the   middle   on the left   probably   you can see

A: What are you doing?
B: I'm looking at a book about festivals. The photographs are great. Look at this one.
A: Where is it?
B: I'm not sure. [1] _Maybe_ it's in Spain [2]_____ it's hot and sunny.
A: Look at the woman in the [3]_____ of the photo. She's playing the guitar.
B: Yes. And the woman [4]_____ is singing.
A: It's [5]_____ a big party.
B: Well, it's [6]_____ a festival. The women [7]_____ foreground look happy.
A: Yes, and [8]_____ people dancing in the background. They're definitely having a good time.

2 Match the words (1–5) with sentences (a–e).

1 a parade _b_
2 In the background ___
3 a celebration ___
4 you can see ___
5 Perhaps ___

a It's **like a big party** for Chinese New Year.
b There's **a sort of walk** with music.
c **Maybe** it's in China because you can see Chinese shops in the background.
d In the background **there are** people watching the parade.
e **Behind them** you can see some shops.

3 Write a description of the picture on page 18 of the Students' Book. Answer the questions.

- What are the people doing?
- What are they wearing?
- What can you see in the background?
- Where do you think they are?
- What do you think they're celebrating?

Check Your Progress 2

❶ Freetime Choose the correct words to complete the text.

My brother and I are very different. He enjoys ¹*collecting/collect* stamps and coins. He ²*doesn't/also* likes making model aeroplanes ³*for/because* it's creative and it's something he can do on his own. I think it's boring. I'm really ⁴*into/enjoy* sport. I like surfing and skateboarding and I'd like ⁵*the/to* try free running one day. I also like ⁶*dancing/to dance* and singing. My brother ⁷*don't/doesn't* enjoy going out. He prefers ⁸*playing/watching* computer games at home. I ⁹*'d like to play/like playing* the air guitar.

/9

❷ Present Perfect (1) Complete the replies with the correct form of the verbs in brackets.

1 You look sad. → I _____ with my boyfriend. (finish)
2 Your hair looks nice. → Thanks. I _____ it with a new shampoo. (wash)
3 I can't open it. → _____ you _____ the right password? (put in)
4 Where's Wally? → I don't know, I _____ him. (not see)
5 Dan looks worried. → Yes, he _____ his phone. (lose)
6 There isn't any chocolate. → I know, I _____ it all. (eat)
7 Laura looks happy. → Yes, she _____ her English test. (pass)
8 I can't find my camera. → _____ you _____ in your school bag? (look)

/8

❸ Modifiers Choose the correct modifier to complete the sentences.

1 Charlie Chaplin films are *really/very* great.
2 Photography is *really/absolutely* interesting.
3 Collecting stamps is *absolutely/a bit* boring.
4 Chess is *quite/absolutely* difficult.
5 Yoga is *very/a bit* relaxing.
6 *Take That* are *absolutely/very* amazing.
7 The *Sims* is *absolutely/very* good.
8 My English pronunciation is *a bit/absolutely* perfect.

/8

❹ Some, any, no, a lot of, a few, a little Cross out the quantifier that is *not possible* in each sentence.

1 I speak *some/any/a little* French.
2 I have *no/some/any* money.
3 Bill knows *a lot of/a few/a little* people.
4 I don't eat *some/any/a lot of* fish.
5 There are *a few/no/any* boys here.
6 Is there *any/a few/a little* juice in the fridge?
7 Please give me *a little/some/any* time.
8 I don't have *a lot of/any/some* luck.
9 There aren't *any/some* people in the park.
10 I need *a/some* money to buy a music DVD.

/10

TOTAL SCORE /35

Module Diary

❶ **Look at the objectives on page 13 in the Students' Book. Choose three and evaluate your learning.**

1 Now I can _____
  well / quite well / with problems.
2 Now I can _____
  well / quite well / with problems.
3 Now I can _____
  well / quite well / with problems.

❷ **Look at your results. What language areas in this module do you need to study more?**

Exam Choice 1

Reading

1 Read about Bastille Day. Match the headings (a-f) with the paragraphs (1-5). There is one extra heading.

a The Fireman's Ball
b The origins of Bastille Day
c American independence
d A national celebration
e A party at the palace
f Parades

Bastille Day

1 ___ Bastille Day is a big celebration in France on 14 July each year. It's like Independence Day in the USA because it is a celebration of the beginning of a new kind of <u>government</u> and is also a national holiday.

2 ___ The Bastille was a prison in Paris where the French royal family <u>locked up</u> anybody who disagreed with them. On 14 July 1789 a large number of French <u>citizens</u> attacked the Bastille. It was the beginning of the French revolution.

3 ___ On the morning of 14 July, parades <u>take place</u> all over the country. The most important parade is on the Champs Elysees in the centre of Paris. Soldiers and police parade in their <u>uniforms</u> and the <u>band</u> plays music.

4 ___ The President of the Republic of France watches the parade and then has a garden party at the Elysee Palace. At night thousands of people watch a wonderful <u>firework display</u> under the Eiffel Tower.

5 ___ Parties take place all over France on Bastille Day, but the best party in Paris is 'The Fireman's Ball'. Fire stations are party <u>venues</u> for the night. People go there to dance all night.

2 Match the <u>underlined</u> words in the text with the meanings (1-8).

1 a show of exploding objects that produce coloured lights in the sky – _____
2 people who live in a particular town or country – _____
3 a group of musicians who play music together – _____
4 the group of people who control a country – _____
5 to happen or to occur – _____
6 places where events happen – _____
7 sets of clothes that police and the army wear so that they all look the same – _____
8 put someone in prison – _____

Listening

3 〔**1.11**〕 **Listen to five short conversations. Choose the correct answer.**

1 Where is Sue?

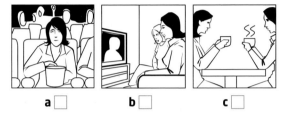

a ☐   b ☐   c ☐

2 What does Bev always have for lunch?

a ☐   b ☐   c ☐

3 Which picture is Joe describing?

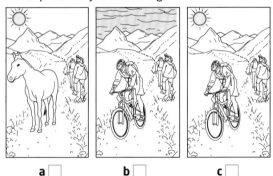

a ☐   b ☐   c ☐

4 What time does Frank usually go to sleep?

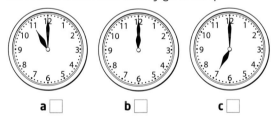

a ☐   b ☐   c ☐

5 Which message does Mrs James give Mark?

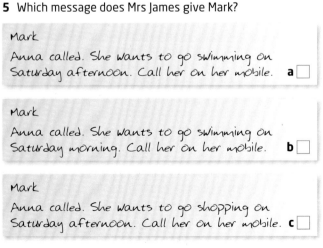

Mark
Anna called. She wants to go swimming on Saturday afternoon. Call her on her mobile. **a** ☐

Mark
Anna called. She wants to go swimming on Saturday morning. Call her on her mobile. **b** ☐

Mark
Anna called. She wants to go shopping on Saturday afternoon. Call her on her mobile. **c** ☐

4 〔**1.12**〕 **Listen to Jack talking to Anna about hobbies. Match the people to the hobbies. There are two extra hobbies.**

1 Anna   ☐ ☐
2 Jack   ☐
3 Teresa   ☐
4 Linda   ☐
5 Martin   ☐

a gymnastics
b photography
c free running
d sailing
e urban dance
f piano
g fashion
h cycling

Speaking

5 **Complete the dialogue with the correct words.**

A: Hi, Mrs Smith. It's Anna. ¹M_____ I speak to Matt please?

B: Hi, Anna. Sorry, but Matt's ²o_____. Do you want to leave a ³m_____?

A: Oh yes please. I want to go on a fun run on Saturday. It's ⁴l_____ a race but you have to pay to take part in it. We're raising money for the school.

B: That's a great idea.

A: Anyway, it starts at ten o'clock. Can Matt phone me ⁵a_____ it?

B: Okay, I'll give him the message.

A: Thanks Mrs Smith.

B: Not ⁶a_____ all.

6 〔**1.13**〕 **Listen, check and repeat.**

Exam Choice 1

Use of English

7 Read about free time and choose the correct answers.

In my free time, I go free running. I do it
¹_____ the weekend. I like football too
²_____ I don't play it now. I haven't got
much time because we get ³_____ of
homework at school.
I also like ⁴_____ photography. I like taking
photographs when I'm on holiday. ⁵_____ of
them are quite good – they're on my website
if you want to see them. It's not a very good
website because I ⁶_____ learned much
about making websites but I enjoy trying.
My favourite photo is of my brother at a
concert. In the photo, he ⁷_____ the air
guitar and he looks really funny. ⁸_____
the background, you can see the band. They
⁹_____ at him. I think they like him! My
brother is very happy now because he
¹⁰_____ his own band. They aren't very
good but they make a lot of noise!

1 a on	**b** at	**c** in
2 a but	**b** and	**c** or
3 a a few	**b** a lot	**c** some
4 a playing	**b** going	**c** doing
5 a Any	**b** A little	**c** Some
6 a don't	**b** haven't	**c** am not
7 a is playing	**b** plays	**c** has played
8 a On	**b** At	**c** In
9 a look	**b** are looking	**c** have looked
10 a has started	**b** starts	**c** is starting

Writing

8 Use the linkers in brackets to join the sentences. Leave out words where possible.

1 In the evening I have dinner with my family. I do my homework. (and then)
In the evening I have dinner with my family and then I do my homework.

2 On Saturdays my father goes to the gym. He sometimes goes to the swimming pool. (or)
_____

3 My sister is very musical – she plays the guitar. She also plays the piano. (and)
_____

4 I love fruit and vegetables. I don't like meat. (but)
_____

5 My mother does the housework in the morning. She goes to work in the afternoon. (and then)
_____

6 My friends come to my house and we play computer games. We sometimes watch a DVD. (or)
_____

7 I want to study English at university. My parents want me to study maths. (but)
_____

9 Complete the email from a French boy who lives in Paris. Use linkers and purpose linkers.

From:	Emile
To:	Ben

Dear Ben

I'm writing ¹___to___ invite you to come to Paris in July. It's very hot ²_____ sunny here, and on the 14 July we have a party ³_____ celebrate Bastille Day. It's really good fun.
During the day, I go to the city centre with my brothers Michel ⁴_____ Jean. We watch a parade and ⁵_____ we listen to the President's speech. On Bastille Day I love the fireworks, ⁶_____ my dog, Max, hates them, so he stays at home.
Thousands of tourists come to Paris ⁷_____ the summer holidays. Most French people usually leave the city in July and August because they prefer to go to the beach ⁸_____ the mountains.
I hope you can come – you'll love Paris.

Emile

TOPIC TALK – VOCABULARY

1 Match a word from column A with a word from column B to make another word.

1 bank _c_   a money
2 charity ___   b job
3 street ___   c account
4 part-time ___   d market
5 pocket ___   e centre
6 shopping ___   f shop

2 Match the words from Exercise 1 with the clues (1-6).

1 You put money in this. __bank account__
2 You don't work here all the time. _____
3 You can buy cheap, second-hand things here. _____
4 You get this from your parents (if you're lucky!). _____
5 You find lots of different shops and restaurants here. _____
6 You can buy cheap food or clothes here. It's outside. _____

3 Complete the dialogues with the words below.

calls   CDs   downloads   drink   ~~games~~   out
present   cosmetics   second-hand

1 **A:** Do you spend a lot of money on computer _games_ ?
   B: No, I prefer to spend my money on going _____.
2 **A:** What _____ do you buy?
   B: Not many, just some make-up. My parents buy shampoo and soap.
3 **A:** Do you ever buy _____ clothes?
   B: Yes, I do. Sometimes, they're really cheap.
4 **A:** What do you spend most of your money on?
   B: Mobile phone _____. I spend all my pocket money on them.
5 **A:** Do you ever pay for music _____ from the internet?
   B: No, I prefer to buy _____ from shops. I like to look at them in my bedroom.
6 **A:** You usually spend lots of money on food and _____. Are you on a diet?
   B: No. I'm trying to save some money to buy a _____ for my mum's birthday.

4 <u>Underline</u> the correct prepositions.

1 I'm very good (with)/for money.
2 I don't spend any money on/for music or going out.
3 I enjoy shopping at/on discount shops or online.
4 I earn a lot of money for/from my part-time job.
5 I put all my money at/in my bank account.

5 Match the verbs (1-5) with the phrases (a-e) and write sentences.

1 earn money _c_   a by looking for bargains
2 get money ___   b in my bank account
3 put money ___   c from my part-time job
4 save money ___   d on clothes and going out
5 spend money ___   e from my parents

I earn money from my part-time job in a shop.
_____
_____
_____
_____

6 Complete the text with the words below.

downloads   get   charity   bank account   spend
~~quite~~   books   online   part-time   earn

I'm [1] _quite_ good with money. I [2]_____ £5 a week pocket money and I [3]_____ £15 a week from a [4]_____ job. I save £10 a month and put it in my [5]_____. I [6]_____ money on music [7]_____ and second-hand [8]_____. I enjoy shopping in [9]_____ shops and sometimes shop [10]_____.

7 Complete the text with the correct words.

My brother isn't very [1] _good_ with money. He [2]_____ £40 a week from a part-time [3]_____ and he gets £75 [4]_____ month pocket money from mum. The problem is that he enjoys shopping [5]_____ shopping centres too much. He [6]_____ all his money on music, clothes and cosmetics. I know he has a bank [7]_____ but he never [8]_____ any money in it. In fact, I don't think he knows where the bank is!

Reading

1 **Read the blog. Are the sentences true (T) or false (F)?**

1 Amy goes to an expensive gym. ___
2 Billy wanted to buy a desk online. ___
3 Freecycling is an online furniture shop. ___

4 Rani is worried about the environment. ___
5 Martin's father is mean. ___
6 Julie hates shopping. ___

MISS FRUGAL'S money-saving blog

We asked you to send us your money-saving tips and stories. Here's a selection of the best.

POSTED: 1 min ago

Amy, London
I like to keep fit but I don't want to fork out on an expensive gym. Everything's expensive in London, but there are lots of parks. So I bought ¹**some** running shoes, and started to go running in the park. I also walk to school now. I save money and get fit at the same time.

POSTED: 3 mins ago

Billy, Southampton
I wanted to change my bedroom and get a new desk, so I was checking out prices of bedroom furniture online when I found a website called Freecycle. Freecycling is when a person gives away things they don't need. I found a perfect small wooden desk for my bedroom, and it was free!

POSTED: 7 mins ago

Rani, Bristol
Every time I go to a supermarket, I get a plastic bag. Every time I do exercise I have ²**some** water. Every time I go to a restaurant I have ³**some** cola. In future, I'm going to buy a 'Bag for Life' and drink tap water. I'll save money, and help the environment too.

POSTED: 8 mins ago

Martin, Cardiff
My father earns a lot of money, and he saves most of it, but he isn't mean. He buys my mum ⁴**some** flowers every Friday, and when he travels, he always brings mum ⁵**some** perfume and ⁶**some** chocolates. But he has taught us to be quite frugal. His advice is, when you want to buy something, ask yourself two questions. First, do you really need it? And secondly, can you get it cheaper somewhere else?

POSTED: 9 mins ago

Julie
I love designer clothes and the latest fashions, and I really want a cool pair of Gucci sunglasses. I need to save money, so here's ⁷**some** advice for people like me – don't go shopping! Don't go to shopping centres, and don't use online shopping sites. They're dangerous!

Word Builder Quantities

2 Read the text again. Replace the <u>underlined</u> words (1-7) with the phrases (a-f) below.

a a pair of _____1_____
b a bouquet of _____
c a bit of _____
d a bottle of (x 2) _____
e a box of _____
f a can of _____

3 Complete the text with the correct words.

It was my girlfriend's birthday last month but I only had ¹ _a bit of_ money. So, instead of doing something expensive I surprised her with ² _____ roses (from my grandma's garden!) and we went to the park and had ³ _____ lemonade and ⁴ _____ crisps. I took ⁵ _____ matches and lit a candle on a chocolate bar! It was just ⁶ _____ fun and she was really pleased I remembered.

Sentence Builder Adjective Order

4 Choose the correct words to complete the sentences.

1 I love your _new sports_/sports new bag.
2 I've lost my _old brown leather/brown old leather_ wallet.
3 She wore her _amazing big red/big amazing red_ hat to the wedding.
4 I want a _new nice school/nice new school_ bag.
5 She usually wears _designer expensive/expensive designer_ jeans.

5 Complete the sentences with the words in the correct order.

1 What are you doing with that _dirty second-hand_ book? (second-hand / dirty)
2 My brother bought an _____ mobile phone. (new / expensive / silver)
3 I gave my mum a _____ bouquet of flowers – she was really pleased. (red / big / beautiful)
4 Did you see her? She was wearing a _____ dress. (purple / Versace / lovely)
5 Look, there's a really _____ denim jeans in this magazine. (black / pair of / nice / men's)

Writing

6 Write an advert for something you own.

- What is the price?
- What is it?
- Can you describe it?
- Is it new or second hand?
- Is it in good condition?
- What are your contact details?

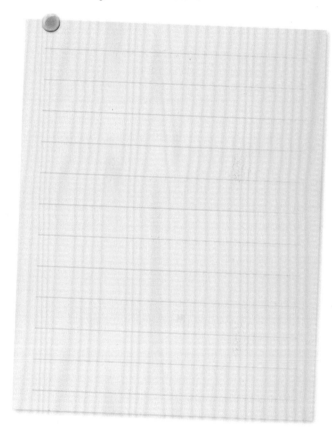

GRAMMAR
Present Perfect (2)

REMEMBER

Complete exercises A–C before you start this lesson.

A Write the 3rd form of the verbs. <u>Underline</u> the regular verb on each line.

1 climb _climbed_ steal _____ sell _____ spend _____

2 eat _____ have _____ make _____ stop _____

3 forget _____ ring _____ take _____ decide _____

4 choose _____ pay _____ try _____ write _____

B Write positive or negative sentences. Use the Present Perfect.

1 I / sell / clothes on eBay.
   + _I've sold clothes on eBay._

2 I / buy / a second-hand English dictionary.
   – _____

3 I / spend / all this month's pocket money.
   – _____

4 My mum / buy / a new dress.
   + _____

5 My dad / give / his old laptop to me.
   + _____

6 I / save 200 euros / for a new bike.
   + _____

C Use the cues to write questions and answers in the Present Perfect and *ever*.

1 you / buy / clothes from a second-hand shop? ✔
   Have you ever bought clothes from a
   second-hand shop?
   Yes, I have.

2 you / have a holiday / in the USA? ✘
   _____
   _____

3 your dad / eat / a burger? ✔
   _____
   _____

4 you / earn / more than a 100 euros in a day? ✘
   _____
   _____

5 it / snow / in your city? ✔
   _____
   _____

1 * Complete the sentences with the correct form of the verbs in brackets.

1 I _'ve found_ (find) a good website for music downloads.

2 My parents _____ (go) skiing.

3 I _____ (not put) my birthday money in the bank.

4 My mum _____ (give) me her old phone.

5 I _____ (not meet) the love of my life.

6 My dad _____ (find) a car that he likes but he _____ (not buy) it yet.

7 Can we watch a different DVD? I _____ (see) this one.

8 I _____ (always want) to go to Forbidden Planet.

Sentence Builder *ever/never*

2 ** Complete the questions and sentences with the word *ever* or *never* in the correct places.

1 Have you ~~ever~~ downloaded music from the internet?

2 I have earned more than €50 a week.

3 Have you used make-up?

4 My brother has saved anything.

5 My dad has bought any second-hand clothes.

6 Has your mum sold anything on eBay?

3 Use the cues to write question and answers.

1 part-time / I / had / a / job. / never / have
   _____ _I have never had a part-time job._ _____

2 has / sister / never / money. / earned / My / any
   _____

3 seen / ever / you / Have / *Star Wars*?
   _____

4 mum / you / ever / Has / given / pocket money? / your
   _____

5 shopping centres. / has / never / shopping / at / enjoyed / He
   _____

Sentence Builder *already/yet*

4 ** Use the cues to write questions and answers in the Present Perfect. Use *already* and *yet*.

1 A: pass your driving test?
  B: start taking lessons
  A: *Have you passed your driving test, yet?*
  B: *No, I haven't. But I've already started taking lessons.*

2 A: read *Macbeth*?
  B: see the play
  A: _____
  B: _____

3 A: buy the new Radiohead album?
  B: listen to it online
  A: _____
  B: _____

4 A: sell your old laptop?
  B: put it on eBay
  A: _____
  B: _____

5 A: find a birthday present for mum?
  B: buy her a card
  A: _____
  B: _____

5 *** Use the cues to write questions and sentences. Use the Present Perfect. Use a time adverb (*ever, never, yet, already*) in the correct place if there is a (T) at the end of the sentence.

1 Ebooks / not become / more popular than books (T)
Ebooks haven't become more popular than books yet.

2 I / see / lots of films at this cinema
_____

3 you / buy / clothes for your mum for her birthday? (T)
_____

4 I / have / a summer job because I don't like working in the holidays (T)
_____

5 I can't buy anything because I / spend / all my money (T)
_____

6 My mum / not give me / my pocket money (T)
_____

Grammar Alive Experiences

6 ** Use the cues to write questions and answers.

- go to Paris? ✔ (four times)
- see a live band ✗ (but watched lots online)
- ride a motorbike ✗ (but driven a car)
- sleep in a tent ✔ (on a school trip)
- earn money ✗ (but would like a part-time job)
- do salsa dancing ✗ (but eaten salsa sauce!)
- cook a meal for your parents ✔ (lots of times)

1 *Have you ever been to Paris?*
Yes, I have. I've been to Paris four times.

2 _____
_____

3 _____
_____

4 _____
_____

5 _____
_____

6 _____
_____

7 _____
_____

1 <u>Underline</u> one incorrect item in each category. Put them in the correct category.

Antiques
an 18th century painting, a 1920s dress, <u>a pair of headphones</u>, a Roman coin, an 18th century Turkish carpet _____

Electronic goods
second-hand clothes, a box of DVDs, CDs, videos _____

Food and drink
a chicken, a bowl, a kilogram of mushrooms, a pineapple _____

Clothes
a jacket, scarves, a pair of jeans, a top _____

Accessories
a bracelet, a necklace, an 18th century Turkish carpet, a pair of boots _____

Arts and crafts
a vase, a modern painting, a teapot, spices _____

2 [1.14] Match the sentences from the dialogue. Listen and check your answers.

1 Can I _d_
2 What ___
3 Can I try ___
4 The changing room ___
5 It's a bit ___
6 What about ___
7 Can ___

a I help you?
b too big.
c a scarf?
d have this one please?
e it on please?
f size?
g is over there.

3 [1.15] Complete the dialogue with the correct words. Then listen and check your answers.

Luke: Let's go to the antiques market. I love looking at old things.

Kelly: Me too. It's mum's birthday next week. Let's choose a present for her.

Luke: Sure. Let's go.

Assistant: ¹*Can I*/*I will* help you?

Kelly: Oh yes. ²*Could you/Can I* have a look at that bracelet please?

Assistant: Here you are.

Kelly: Hmm I think it's ³*about/a bit* too big for mum.

Assistant: What about this one? It's similar, but smaller.

Kelly: ⁴*What about/Can I* try it on?

Assistant: Yes of course.

Kelly: ⁵*How much/How many* is it?

Assistant: £20.

Kelly: Oh, it's too expensive.

Assistant: It's silver, but you can have it for £18.50.

Luke: Okay, great. Here you are.

Assistant: ⁶*That's/Take* one pound fifty change.

Luke: Could you wrap it up, ⁷*madam/please*? It's for a present.

Assistant: Sure. Here you are.

4 You are at a clothes market with a friend. Choose something to buy from the words below. Use the phrases from Exercise 2 to write a dialogue.

a hat   a scarf   a dress   a pair of boots   a handbag   a bracelet   a jacket

A: _____ _____ _____
B: _____ _____ _____
A: _____ _____ _____
B: _____ _____ _____
A: _____ _____ _____

Check Your Progress 3

❶ Money Complete the text with the correct words.

How to be good with money: If you get pocket money or earn money ¹_____ a part-time job, don't spend it all ²_____ silly things that you don't really need. Each month try to put some ³_____ your bank account. Begin with something small – £20 ⁴_____ month. Also, don't shop ⁵_____ expensive shopping centres. Look for bargains ⁶_____ charity shops or discount shops. It's amazing what you can find. I enjoy ⁷_____ at second-hand shops.

/7

❷ Quantities Underline the word that is *not* possible in each line.

1 I'd like a bit of *advice/information/chocolates*.
2 She bought me a bottle of *aftershave/sweets/cola*.
3 He gave her a beautiful bouquet of *perfume/roses/flowers*.
4 She's wearing a new pair of *shoes/jeans/clothes*.
5 Can I have three packets of *orange juice/crisps/biscuits* please?
6 Where's the box of *chocolates/beans/matches*?
7 Could I have a bit of *crisps/chocolate/bread*?

/7

❸ Present Perfect Complete the sentences with the Present Perfect form of the words in brackets.

1 Peter _____ (never save) any money in his life.
2 _____ (you / spend) a lot of money on clothes and shoes?
3 Jane _____ (never buy) anything online.
4 Lily _____ (sell) lots of things on the internet.
5 We _____ (not give) her any money for her birthday.
6 _____ (Tom ever earn) any money?
7 Dad _____ (not go) to the market today.
8 _____ (you / see) the new second-hand shop in town?

/8

❹ Present Perfect Use the cues to write sentences and questions. Use the words below.

already   ever   yet   never

1 you / visit / Iceland?
   _____
2 I'm not hungry, thanks. I / eat
   _____
3 Rob doesn't drive. He / not pass / test
   _____
4 you / find / your mobile phone?
   _____
5 I / won / any money
   _____
6 Debbie / not receive / exam results
   _____

/6

❺ Shopping Complete the dialogue with the correct words.

A: Can I ¹_____ you?
B: Yes, can I have a ²_____ at that scarf, please?
A: Yes, of course.
B: How ³_____ is it?
A: Ten pounds.
B: It's a bit too ⁴_____.
A: Okay. ⁵_____ one is eight pounds.
B: Okay. ⁶_____ you wrap it up, please?
A: I'm ⁷_____. I haven't got any paper.

/7

TOTAL SCORE */35*

Module Diary

❶ Look at the objectives on page 21 in the Students' Book. Choose three and evaluate your learning.

1 Now I can _____
   well / quite well / with problems.
2 Now I can _____
   well / quite well / with problems.
3 Now I can _____
   well / quite well / with problems.

❷ Look at your results. What language areas in this module do you need to study more?

Sound Choice 2

Sound Check

Say the words and expressions below.

a began / begun (Exercises 1 and 2)
b Sue / shoes (Exercise 3)
c right / write / seen / scene (Exercises 4 and 5)
d Could I look at that please? (Exercise 6)
e bracelet / celebrate (Exercise 7)

1.16 **Listen and check your answers. Which sounds and expressions did you have problems with? Choose three exercises to do below.**

1 **1.17** Grammar - irregular verbs **Complete the table with the second and third forms of the verbs. Listen, check and repeat.**

1st form	2nd form	3rd form
begin	*began*	*begun*
drink		
ring		
sing		
sink		
swim		

2 **1.18** Grammar - contractions **Listen and repeat.**

1 I've never been to Paris.
2 They've drunk all the milk!
3 He's played for that football team for years.
4 She hasn't sung my favourite song yet.
5 She hasn't swum in the sea.
6 We've seen that film lots of times.

3 **1.19** Consonants - /ʃ/ and /s/ **Listen and repeat the tongue twisters.**

1 Sheila showed Shaun some shorts, shirts and shoes in her shop.
2 Sam sold Sue some super second-hand silver sunglasses.

4 **1.20** Vowels and spelling - /iː/ and /aɪ/ **Match the words with the same sound. Then listen, check and repeat.**

1 buy _c_
2 peace ___
3 right ___
4 scene ___

a piece
b seen
c bye
d write

5 **1.21** Vowels and spelling - /iː/ and /aɪ/. **Match the words to the correct sound. Then listen, check and repeat.**

clean ~~high~~ leave meet mile
shy size sweet

/aɪ/ buy bye right write
___*high*___ _____ _____ _____
/iː/ peace piece scene seen
_____ _____ _____ _____

6 **1.22** Expressions **Listen and underline the two stressed words or syllables on each line. Listen again and repeat.**

A I'd like to try gymnastics.
I'm really into dancing.
I do it every weekend.
I like it because it's fun.

B Could I look at that please?
Can I try it on please?
Could you wrap it up please?
Thank you very much.

7 **1.23** Difficult words **Put the words into the correct column. Listen and repeat.**

argument ~~bracelet~~ celebrate chocolate library
opera restaurant valuable

■■.	■.■.
bracelet	

28

TOPIC TALK – VOCABULARY

1 Complete the puzzle with film types. What is the hidden word?

1 Exciting. Usually about crime.
2 About police and criminals.
3 Often scary. About dead people you can see.
4 Very exciting and sometimes dangerous stories.
5 Set in nineteenth century USA. Guns and horses.
6 Very scary or shocking. Sometimes lots of blood.
7 Imagining the future or other planets.
8 A type of policeman tries to solve a crime.
9 The opposite to real life.
10 About relationships and romance.

1 t h r i l l e r

2 Complete the sentences with the words below.

~~boring~~ depressing funny imaginative interesting romantic violent

1 It was really _boring_, the story wasn't interesting.
2 It was really _____, I laughed and laughed.
3 It was really _____, there was a lot of fighting and killing.
4 It was really _____, there were a lot of incredible new ideas.
5 It was really _____, I felt really sad about the future.
6 It was really _____, the main characters were really in love.
7 It was really _____, I learnt so much about animals from the story.

3 Choose the best answer to the questions.

One of my ¹___a___ books is *The Day of the Jackal* ²_____ Frederick Forsyth. It's a detective ³_____ but it's also ⁴_____ thriller. The story ⁵_____ place in France during the 1960s. It's ⁶_____ a plan to kill the French President, General de Gaulle. A secret organisation hire a professional – 'The Jackal' – to kill de Gaulle and police detective Claude Lebel tries to stop him. It's really ⁷_____ and I couldn't put it down.

PENGUIN READERS

The Day of the Jackal
Frederick Forsyth

1	**a** favourite	**b** love	**c** bestseller
2	**a** for	**b** under	**c** by
3	**a** story	**b** crime	**c** book
4	**a** the	**b** a	**c** -
5	**a** take	**b** takes	**c** have
6	**a** about	**b** on	**c** for
7	**a** boring	**b** romantic	**c** exciting

GRAMMAR
Past Simple and Continuous

Complete exercises A–C before you start this lesson.

A **Complete the sentences with the Past Simple form of the verbs in brackets.**

1 My parents __*met*__ at university. (meet)
2 I _____ in 1999, I _____ in 1998. (not be born / be born)
3 My dad _____ a new laptop yesterday. (buy)
4 I _____ last night, I _____. (not go out / stay at home)
5 I _____ at 7.30 this morning. (get up)
6 I _____ lunch with my family. (have)
7 I _____ pizza and salad for lunch yesteday. (eat)
8 I _____ the football match on TV because I was busy. (not watch)

B **Write questions to the answers in Exercise A.**

1 Where __*did your parents meet*__?
2 Were _____ 1999?
3 What _____?
4 Did _____?
5 What time _____?
6 Who _____?
7 What _____?
8 Did _____?

C **Complete the text with the Past Simple form of the verbs in brackets.**

Last month, our school [1]__*had*__ (have) an idea to make money for charity. They [2]_____ (ask) everyone to bring old clothes, books and CDs to school to sell. I [3]_____ (decide) to go to school early to help put everything nicely on tables in the hall. I [4]_____ (go) there at two o'clock and [5]_____ (start) working. I [6]_____ (see) a really nice shirt so I [7]_____ (give) a teacher some money for it. Then I [8]_____ (find) a jacket, a coat, some CDs and some books. I [9]_____ (spend) £20 before my friends [10]_____ (arrive). Now, everyone wants to help next year so they can find things before anyone else.

1 * **Complete the sentences about John's day using the Past Continuous.**

1 At 7.30 a.m., I / have breakfast
   At 7.30 a.m., ___*I was having breakfast.*___
2 At 8.30 a.m., I / walk to school
   At 8.30 a.m., _____
3 At 10.00 a.m., my friends / play football
   At 10.00 a.m., _____
4 I not / play because I've got a bad leg
   _____
5 At 12.00, my friends and I / have lunch
   At 12.00, _____
6 At 3.00 p.m., I / have a history lesson
   At 3.00 p.m., _____
7 At 6.00 p.m., I / do my homework, my sister / make dinner and my parents / watch television
   At 6.00 p.m., _____
8 At 8.00 p.m., I / play computer games
   At 8.00 p.m., _____

2 ** Use the cues to write questions and short answers about John's day yesterday in the Past Continuous.

1 John / have breakfast at 7.00 a.m. yesterday? ✔
Was John having breakfast at 7.00 a.m. yesterday?
Yes, he was.

2 What / John / do at 8.30 a.m.?
_____

He was walking to school.

3 John / play football at 10.00 a.m.? ✘
_____
_____

4 What / John and his friends / do at 12.00?
_____

They were having lunch.

5 John / geography lesson at 3.00 p.m.? ✘
_____
_____

6 John / do his homework at 6.00 p.m.? ✔
_____
_____

7 John's parents / work at 6 p.m.? ✘
_____
_____

8 Who / make dinner at 6 p.m.?
_____

John's sister.

9 John / watch TV at 8.00 p.m.?
_____
_____

3 ** Choose the correct words to complete the sentences.

1 I *waited/was waiting* for a taxi when I saw my friend.

2 It *rained/was raining* when I left the house.

3 I was lying in bed when I *heard/was hearing* a strange noise.

4 When we *arrived/were arriving* home from Egypt, we *still wore/were still wearing* T-shirts and shorts. We were freezing!

5 I *looked/was looking* at some old photos when I *found/was finding* one of my dad when he was seventeen. He *had/was having* really long hair.

6 My friend *talked/was talking* on his mobile phone so I *didn't say/wasn't saying* anything to him.

7 I *was cooking/cooked* dinner when my friend *arrived/was arriving* at my house.

4 *** Complete the text with the verbs below. Use the Past Simple or Past Continuous.

look   not wear   see   stand   tell   think
~~wait~~   walk

I was going on holiday and my flight was leaving from Heathrow airport. I ¹ _was waiting_ in the airport terminal when I ² _____ a man. He ³ _____ near a computer shop. He was strange because he ⁴ _____ modern clothes, but a big hat and long boots. He ⁵ _____ like someone from the 18ᵗʰ century. I ⁶ _____ he was wearing fancy dress. After a few moments, he ⁷ _____ away, and disappeared. Later, someone ⁸ _____ me that there are several ghosts at Heathrow airport.

Grammar Alive Telling an anecdote

5 *** Choose A, B or C and use the cues to write a short anecdote.

A camp in the mountains - try to sleep - hear a strange noise - very scared - look out the tent - see three cows

B walk to the bus stop - drop my keys - can't see them anywhere - finally find them - miss the bus

C sit in the park - eat my sandwiches - notice a man - he look at me and smile - we wear exactly the same T-shirt

A *We were camping in the mountains. We were trying to sleep when we …*

Listening

1 ▸ 1.24 **Listen to a conversation between two friends, Sarah and Duncan. Choose the best answer to the questions.**

1 What does Sarah think of films about pirates?
a She loves them. **b** She doesn't like them.
c She quite likes them.

2 What sort of story is *Pirates of the Caribbean*?
a a ghost story **b** a historical story
c an adventure story

3 In which century does the *Pirates of the Caribbean* take place?
a seventeenth **b** eightteenth **c** nineteenth

4 What happened when Will Turner first met Elizabeth?
a He saved her life.
b They fell in love.
c She saved his life.

5 What does Duncan think of Johnny Depp?
a He thinks he's a good actor.
b He thinks he's a bad actor.
c He thinks he's okay.

6 What does Sarah think about Keira Knightley?
a She thinks she's a good actor.
b She doesn't think she's a good actor.
c She thinks she's young.

7 What sort of stories does Sarah like?
a crime **b** love **c** historical

8 Why is Mrs Bennet worried about her five daughters?
a because they aren't married
b because their husbands aren't rich
c because they haven't got jobs

Sentence Builder Adjectives and prepositions

2 **Complete the sentences about Sarah and Duncan with the correct words. Are the sentences true (T) or false (F)?**

1 Sarah is afraid ___of___ pirates. ___

2 Duncan thinks Johnny Depp is good _____ playing a pirate. ___

3 Duncan thinks Keira Knightley is bad _____ acting. ___

4 Sarah is interested _____ watching adventure films. ___

5 Mrs Bennet is worried _____ her daughters' future. ___

Word Builder Multi-part verbs (1)

3 **Use the words below to rewrite the underlined phrases.**

a went back **b** went straight **c** sailed back
d picked her up **e** was going back **f** pick her up

The film, *Titanic*, is a love story. After a holiday in Europe a beautiful young woman called Rose [1]was returning _e_ to America with her mother and her rich fiancé, Cal. On the ship, Rose met Jack, a poor artist and they fell in love. Rose had a good time with Jack in 3rd class, but when she [2]returned ___ to first class, Cal was angry. He said Jack stole a necklace. The guards arrested Jack, and soon afterwards the Titanic hit an iceberg and started sinking. Rose [3]went directly ___ to the cabin where Jack was a prisoner and helped him to escape. The Titanic was sinking, and Rose and Jack were in the water. Some people in a small boat saw Rose and [4]collected her, ___ but they left Jack behind. So Rose jumped into the sea because she wanted to stay with Jack. When the boat [5]returned ___ to Rose to [6]collect her ___ again, Jack told her to get in. That was the last time she saw him.

LESSON 12

GRAMMAR
Present Perfect and Past Simple

1 * **Choose the correct words to complete the sentences.**

1 My cousin *has got married/got married* last summer in a hotel.

2 I*'ve already been/already went* to two weddings this year.

3 My mum and dad *have met/met* in the 1990s.

4 I *haven't met/didn't meet* the love of my life yet.

5 My sister says she*'s never fallen/never fell* in love before.

6 My brother and his girlfriend *haven't got on/didn't get on* very well at first.

2 ** **Use the cues to write questions in the Present Perfect or Past Simple.**

1 We went out last night (Where / go?)
   Where did you go?

2 Something has happened (What / happen?)
   _____

3 I've read *The Count of Monte Cristo* a few times (How many times / read it?)
   _____

4 Somebody phoned her before the lesson (Who / phone?)
   _____

5 Jane and I went to see a romantic comedy at the cinema yesterday (What time / go?)
   _____

6 Sarah got married (When / be / the wedding?)
   _____

3 ** **Use the cues to make dialogues.**

1 **A:** visit / Paris? → **B:** Yes →
  A: How long / stay? → **B:** Four days

  A: *Have you ever visited Paris?*
  B: *Yes, I have.*
  A: *How long did you stay?*
  B: *Four days.*

2 **A:** cry / cinema? → **B:** Yes →
  A: Why / cry? → **B:** It was a very sad film
  _____

3 **A:** write / love letter? → **B:** Yes →
  A: Who / write to? → **B:** My ex-boyfriend
  _____

4 *** **Complete the dialogue with the Present Perfect or Past Simple form of the words in brackets.**

Jackie: ¹ _Have_ you _heard_ (hear) about Tom? He ² _____ (meet) someone.

Dan: A girl?

Jackie: Yes, and he ³ _____ (fall) in love. But there's a problem. He ⁴ _____ (see) her on a bus yesterday and he spoke to her, but then he ⁵ _____ (not ask) for her phone number.

Dan: ⁶ _____ he _____ (ask) her name?

Jackie: Yes, but only her first name and it's Ann. I ⁷ _____ (never see) him so unhappy.

Dan: Oh no! Poor Tom. By the way, How ⁸ _____ (meet) Peter?

Jackie: I ⁹ _____ (go) to a party in August and he was there. We ¹⁰ _____ (get engaged) two weeks ago.

Dan: That's great!

Jackie: ¹¹ _____ you _____ (ever fall) in love at first sight?

Dan: Yes, many times. But sadly, nobody ¹² _____ (ever fall) in love with me!

Workshop 2

Writing

1 **Read the letter. Match the parts of the letter (1-5) with the sections (a-e).**

a ending
b story
c introduction
d email information
e informal beginning

2 **Complete the email with the linkers below.**

at first   but then   in the end   later   luckily   ~~suddenly~~

---

1 _d_ **Subject:** the weekend
To: Doramaggs@talnet.com
From: becky@pnet.com

2 ___ Hi Dora

3 ___ I hope you're well. I'm fine. Last weekend, I had a real adventure. I was staying at my aunt and uncle's house and my uncle has a little boat, so I went sailing with my cousins.

4 ___ We were having a great time in the boat when someone **a** _suddenly_ shouted, 'Hello!'. A boy and a girl were standing on a small island and shouting. **b** _____ I thought they were being friendly and I shouted 'Hello,' **c** _____ the boy shouted 'Help!'. We sailed to the island and the boy carried the girl to the boat because her leg was red and swollen. The boy said his sister was climbing on the rocks when she fell. **d** _____, I had my mobile so I called my aunt and she called an ambulance.

We sailed back to the beach and the girl went to hospital. **e** _____, the girl was okay and **f** _____, her parents called to thank us.

5 ___ Write soon, love Becky xxx

---

3 **Write an email of 100-150 words to a friend telling them about an adventure you had.**

Speaking

1 **1.25** **Choose the correct words to complete the dialogue. Then listen and check your answers.**

A: What did you do at the weekend?
B: <u>Er ... well</u>, I stayed at home and watched DVDs. It was boring. What about you?
A: I went to Paris.
B: ¹_Wow!_/Oh no! Did you go alone?
A: No, with my mother. We stayed with her friend.
B: ²_Oh no!/Mm._
A: She works in the Eiffel tower.
B: ³_Really?/Mm._
A: Yes, there's a restaurant on the second floor. She works there. <u>Anyway</u>, on Saturday, Mum and I went on a boat on the River Seine. We had a bit of an adventure.
B: ⁴_Oh no!/Really?_
A: Yes, we were getting on the boat <u>and then</u> I dropped my bag in the river.
B: ⁵_Mm./Oh no!_
A: I was crying. All my money was in the bag. <u>But then</u> a French boy jumped into the river and saved it.
A: ⁶_Wow!/Mm._
B: I was so happy – my mum gave him twenty euros, and I fell in love!

2 **Look at the <u>underlined</u> words in the dialogue in Exercise 1 and find the linkers.**

1 1 linker to go back to the story _Anyway_
2 2 linkers to link two events _____
3 1 linker to hesitate _____

3 **Write a dialogue in your notebook about a weekend away. Use the notes below, or your own ideas.**

a weekend in Venice with your parents - stayed in an expensive hotel - went sightseeing - got lost - met some nice people - took you back to your hotel - parents invited them to visit you at home

Check Your Progress 4

① Adjectives Complete the sentences with the correct words.

1 I love *Pirates of the Caribbean* - it's b_____.
2 Have you heard the g_____ s_____ about Glencoe?
3 The best d_____ stories are about Sherlock Holmes.
4 The *Harry Potter* books have sold millions - it's a b_____.
5 My little sister loves f_____ - her favourite is *Cinderella*.
6 *Avatar* is probably the most i_____ film I've seen.
7 The film was really f_____. We laughed a lot.

/7

② Describing stories Complete the text with the correct words.

My mother loves films by Alfred Hitchcock. Her ¹_____ film is *The Birds*. It's a horror ²_____ and is based on a novel ³_____ Daphne du Maurier. The story takes ⁴_____ in a small town in Northern California. It's ⁵_____ the strange behaviour of the birds in the town. They suddenly begin to attack people! It's ⁶_____ brilliant film but very, very scary!

/6

③ Past Simple and Continuous Complete the text with the correct form of the verbs in brackets.

A few years ago, a young family ¹_____ (move) to a house in Melbourne, Australia. One night, the couple ²_____ (sleep) when their baby son ³_____ (start) crying. The woman woke up and ⁴_____ (prepare) a bottle of milk when suddenly, the crying ⁵_____ (stop). She went back to bed. A few hours later, the baby cried again. This time she went to check. As she opened the door to her son's room, she ⁶_____ (see) a boy sitting on the bed. He ⁷_____ (calm) the baby down. When he saw the woman, he ⁸_____ (disappear). The woman never saw the boy again but the neighbours ⁹_____ (tell) her it was the ghost of a young boy who ¹⁰_____ (die) in the same room eighty years before.

/10

④ Adjectives and prepositions Complete the questions with a preposition.

1 What type of books are you interested _____?
2 Which school subjects are you good _____?
3 What wild animals are you afraid _____?
4 What sort of things do you worry _____?
5 Are there any sports that you are bad _____?
6 Which things are you relaxed _____?

/6

⑤ Present Perfect and Past Simple Complete the sentences with the Present Perfect or Past Simple form of the words in brackets.

1 I _____ (meet) a beautiful girl and now I'm in love.
2 My mum _____ (meet) my dad at university.
3 She _____ (never see) a Harry Potter film but she _____ (read) all the books.
4 I'm hungry. I _____ (not have) anything to eat all day.
5 They _____ (fall) in love at first sight.
6 We _____ (go) on holiday to France last year.

/6

TOTAL SCORE   /35

Module Diary

① Look at the objectives on page 29 in the Students' Book. Choose three and evaluate your learning.

1 Now I can _____
   well / quite well / with problems.
2 Now I can _____
   well / quite well / with problems.
3 Now I can _____
   well / quite well / with problems.

② Look at your results. What language areas in this module do you need to study more?

Exam Choice 2

Reading

1 Read the emails and choose the best title.

a Joe saved Mrs Powell's life.

b Joe saved Bella's life.

c Joe saved Bob's life.

Subject:	You're a hero!
To:	Joe
From:	Pat Powell
Date:	Thursday 11 February

Dear Joe

Thank you for what you did on Wednesday evening. You saved Bella's life. Eating a sweet and laughing at the same time is not a good idea!

Can you come round to our house for lunch on Sunday? I want to buy you a DVD to say thank you – what sort of films do you like? Do you have any favourite actors?

Thanks again and please give my love to your mum and dad. Do they know their son's a hero?

See you on Sunday I hope.

Mrs Powell (Bella's mum)

Subject:	Bella
To:	Bob
From:	Joe
Date:	Thursday 11 February

Hi Bob

What are you up to? I'm doing my homework in the library with Sam, but it's boring.

Something terrible happened yesterday. I was at home, watching a DVD with Bella and she was eating a sweet. Then something funny happened in the film. She laughed and then she made a strange noise. At first I didn't think it was serious but suddenly her face became really red. I realised she couldn't breathe! So I slapped her on the back and luckily the sweet flew across the room. I think I saved her life! In the end, she was fine so we watched the rest of the DVD.

Anyway, see you at school for football on Saturday,

Joe

2 Read the emails again. Are the sentences true (T) or false (F)?

1 Joe and Bella met on Wednesday. ___

2 Mrs Powell has invited Joe to lunch on Sunday. ___

3 Mrs Powell wants to watch a DVD with Joe. ___

4 Joe is doing his homework in his bedroom. ___

5 Joe and Bella were watching a funny film yesterday. ___

6 They didn't watch the whole film ___

Listening

3 🔊 **1.26** **Listen to the conversation between Amy and Matt. Are the sentences true (T) or false (F)?**

1 Matt went to the cinema yesterday evening. ___
2 He saw a film called *The Greek Gods*. ___
3 He didn't enjoy the film. ___
4 The hero of the film is Percy Jackson. ___
5 His father is half human, half god. ___
6 Percy Jackson crosses America to find his mother. ___
7 Amy says she would like to see the film. ___
8 Matt says the film is exciting but it isn't scary. ___

4 🔊 **1.27** **Listen to the second conversation between Amy and Matt and answer the questions.**

1 Where did Amy see the film, *500 Days of Summer*?
2 What kind of film was it?
3 What are the two main characters called?
4 Where does Tom meet Summer?
5 How does he feel about her?
6 What kind of person is Tom?
7 How often does Matt watch romantic films?
8 Does the film have a happy ending?

Speaking

5 🔊 **1.28** **Choose the correct words to complete the dialogue. Then listen and check your answers.**

Ned: Hi Emily! How was your holiday?

Emily: Great - Minorca is wonderful. It was really hot and we spent every day on the beach.

Ned: [1]*Wow!/Oh no!* Lucky you!

Emily: Well, almost every day. I spent one day in hospital.

Ned: [2]*Mm./Really!* Why?

Emily: Well, I was swimming in the sea when I [3]*quickly/suddenly* had a pain on my foot. A jellyfish stung me!

Ned: [4]*Oh no!/Mm.* What did you do?

Emily: Umm, [5]*well/anyway* I got out of the water. [6]*At first/In the end* my foot was a bit red but I didn't think it was very serious. [7]*Luckily/But then* it became really swollen and I couldn't walk.

Ned: Oh no! Was anybody with you?

Emily: No, but [8]*suddenly/luckily*, I had my mobile phone with me so I called my parents and they took me to hospital. [9]*Suddenly/In the end,* the doctor gave me something to put on my foot and it was fine.

Ned: Oh good. A bee stung me on the foot once and the same thing happened. [10]*Er well/Anyway,* did you go in the sea again after that?

Emily: Ha ha! No, I swam in the swimming pool.

Exam Choice 2

Use of English

6 Complete the second sentence with one or two words so that it has the same meaning as the first.

1 Ow! I've got some glass in my foot.
Ow! I've got a _____ of glass in my foot.

2 This is the first time I've bought clothes online.
I've _____ clothes online before.

3 I'm still looking for my phone.
I haven't found my phone _____.

4 I've got a new T-shirt. It's black and it's cool.
I've got a _____ black T-shirt.

5 I love reading science fiction books.
I'm really interested _____ science fiction.

6 When did you arrive in Greece?
When did you _____ to Greece?

7 My grandfather lived in Egypt for a year but he's never returned there.
My grandfather has never gone _____ to Egypt.

8 I went to Canada last year, three years ago and five years ago.
I've _____ to Canada three times.

9 I started my exam at ten o'clock.
At ten o'clock I _____ starting my exam.

10 Natalie is a great skier.
Natalie is very good _____ skiing.

Writing

7 Complete the sentences using the adjectives in brackets in the correct order.

1 (long / black) some _____ boots
2 (new / cool) a _____ laptop
3 (black / short) a _____ t-shirt
4 (new / fantastic) a _____ MP3 player
5 (man's / blue) a _____ sweater
6 (big / nice) some _____ sunglasses
7 (leather / green) a _____ wallet
8 (sports / leather) a _____ bag

8 Put the lines of an advert in order.

a Secondhand leather jacket ___
b FOR SALE £30 ___
c Contact Ben on 079321100 ___
d This small brown leather jacket is in excellent condition. ___
e It isn't new, but it's still really cool. ___

9 Write an advert for one of these objects.

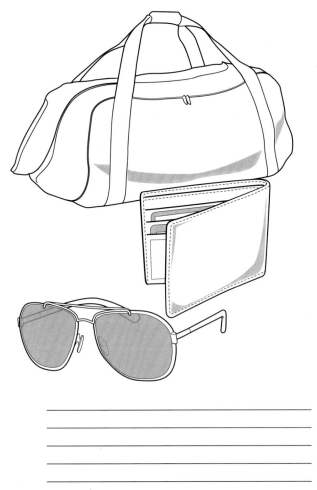

_____
_____
_____
_____
_____
_____

GENERATIONS

TOPIC TALK – VOCABULARY

1 Read the information and match the names of people with how they are related to Barack Obama.

Barack Obama has a very large family. His father, Barack Obama Sr, got married when he was eighteen to a woman called Kezia. They had two children, a son, Malik and a daughter, Auma. Barack Obama Sr later came to Hawaii where he met Ann Dunham. They got married and had a child, Barack Obama Jr, who is now President of the United States. His mother's parents, Stanley and Madelyn looked after Barack for a year when he was young. Barack's mother married for a second time in Indonesia. Her new husband's name was Lolo and they had a daughter, Maya. Barack's wife's name is Michelle. Her father's name is Fraser and her mother's name is Marian. Michelle has one brother, Craig.

brother-in-law   father-in-law   grandparents
half brother   half sisters   mother-in-law
~~parents~~   stepfather

1 Barack Obama Sr and Ann Dunham   _parents_
2 Lolo   _____
3 Auma and Maya   _____
4 Stanley and Madelyn   _____
5 Marian   _____
6 Craig   _____
7 Fraser   _____
8 Malik   _____

2 Complete the descriptions (1–3) with the correct name. Then write a description for the person who is not described.

Debbie   **Viv**   **Angie**   **Flo**

1 _____ is wearing baggy jeans and a jacket with a hood. She's got long hair.
2 _____ is wearing a short dress with leggings. She's got short dyed hair and a piercing above her eye.
3 _____ is wearing a short skirt with leggings and a T-shirt. She's got a tattoo on her left arm.

_____
_____

3 Complete the text with the correct forms of the verbs below.

argue   can't stand   get on   have   have got (x 3)
not often see

I ¹_'ve got_ a big family. I ²_____ two mums and two dads! My parents are divorced, but they got married again, so I've got a stepmother and a stepfather. I ³_____ fours sisters – two are half-sisters and two stepbrothers! I spend a lot of money on birthday presents. I ⁴_____ my father and stepmother because they live in the USA, but I go there for holidays. I ⁵_____ well with my sisters and brothers, but I sometimes ⁶_____ with my stepfather. He ⁷_____ different tastes in fashion and he ⁸_____ my clothes.

1 **Read the blog. What is Zoe's problem?**

a She thinks her mother looks like Madonna.

b She wants a new laptop.

c She doesn't like her mother's clothes.

Teen Advice Blog. Share your worries and opinions with other teens.

Zoe

Posted yesterday at 17:10

MADONNA FAN MOTHER

My problem is my mum! She's really nice and I get on well with her. I sometimes argue with her about little things, but nothing important. All my friends love her – she's great fun. When she was my age, Madonna was really popular and mum was a fan – she wore miniskirts and leggings, lots of jewellery and dyed her hair blond. I think she wanted to be Madonna! She was only sixteen so it was okay. However, she still wears leggings and short denim skirts now, and I can't stand it. She even <u>uploads</u> photos of herself onto her <u>homepage</u>, so all my online friends can see her. What can I do?

Benny

Posted today at 13:21

You're lucky to have a cool mum – my mum is so conservative. She wears baggy jeans and long skirts, and she never wears jewellery. Although she's only thirty-seven, everybody thinks she's older because her clothes are old-fashioned. One friend even thought she was my grandmother! Your mum should give my mum some fashion advice!

Joolee

Posted today at 11:10

I agree with you Zoe. My problem is my father. He loves t-shirts with bad slogans like, 'This is what a cool dad looks like.' :-(

JJR

Posted today at 07:45

I think your mum's cool. But why are you friends with her <u>online</u>??!!?? She's your mother, not your friend!

Zoe

Posted today at 21:01

My mum got me a fantastic new <u>laptop</u> for my birthday, so when she wanted to be my online friend, I couldn't say no! Sometimes, she's at work and I'm at home, and she wants to have a <u>real-time</u> chat with me online! I just go <u>offline</u>. I love chatting to my friends, but I can chat to mum when I get home.

Ross

Posted yesterday at 17:26

Zoe, your mum wants to stay young, and why not? Her generation wore denim miniskirts before our generation. You say she's great fun – that's more important than the clothes she wears. Most parents don't understand the virtual world, but you're lucky – your mother has a homepage and knows how to use it. I think that's great. :-)

2 Read the blog again. Are the sentences true (T) or false (F)?

1 Zoe's friends get on well with her mother. ___
2 Zoe's mother wears normal clothes for her age. ___
3 Benny's mother looks old for her age. ___
4 Joolee's father likes slogans. ___
5 JJR thinks it's okay for Zoe to be online friends with her mother. ___
6 Zoe likes chatting to her mother online. ___
7 Ross thinks Zoe's mother is different from most other parents. ___

Word Builder Compounds

3 Match the underlined words in the text to the definitions below.

1 a portable computer – *laptop*
2 connected to the Net – _____
3 the first page on a website – _____
4 disconnected from the Net – _____
5 put something on the Net – _____
6 in the present – _____

4 Complete the interview with the words below.

page   up   ~~online~~   off   task   top   site   down

A: How many hours do you spend chatting [1] *online* each day?
B: I spend about two hours chatting in real time, but I'm online all the time. I never log [2]_____.
A: What's your favourite [3]web_____?
B: I love YouTube but I love sites about nature.
A: What was the last track you [4]_____ loaded?
B: *Check It Out* by will.i.am.
A: Do you ever multi [5]_____?
B: All the time. I'm doing this interview on my [6]lap _____, texting my friend and [7]_____ loading photos to my home [8]_____ at the same time.

Sentence Builder Contrast linkers

5 Rewrite the sentences using the linking words in brackets.

1 My parents use computers at work. They don't go online to chat or surf the Net for fun. (Although)
Although my parents use computers at work, they don't go online to chat or surf the net for fun.

2 I love downloading music and films on my computer. I prefer playing football to playing computer games. (but)
_____

3 I love Christmas because four generations of our family get together. The teenagers spend hours in front of their computers, and I don't like it. (However)
_____

4 I spend hours on the computer so my parents think I don't have any friends. I have over 200 online friends and I have real-time chats with them all the time. (However)
_____

5 My dad reads the newspaper and watches TV at the same time. He doesn't really multitask. (Although)
_____

Writing

6 Write a blog reply to Bobby65. Use compounds and contrast linkers.

Bobby65

My problem is I sometimes argue with my dad. When he was young he did his homework in his bedroom with no music or TV. He thinks I should do the same and he can't stand it when I do my homework, listen to music and I'm online, too. Although I can understand why he is worrying, I am very good at multitasking and I always do my homework and get good marks. I get on well with my dad, but this is one thing we can't agree on. What can I do?

_____
_____
_____
_____
_____

14

GRAMMAR
Present Perfect (3)

REMEMBER

Complete exercises A–C before you start this lesson.

A Write the third form of the verbs. Then match third forms with the same vowel sound.

1 buy *bought* _c_
2 drive _____ ___
3 know _____ ___
4 make _____ ___
5 mean _____ ___

a show _____
b spend _____
c teach *taught*
d give _____
e pay _____

B Complete the text with the Present Perfect form of the words in brackets.

Hi Jean

Just a quick family update. Jim ¹___ *has just arrived* ___ (just arrive) back from university. I don't think he's getting on very well with his new girlfriend. They ²_____ (have) a few arguments. Katie's fine though. She ³_____ (pass) all her exams this term. Johnny hasn't done very well. He ⁴_____ (not study) much at all. In fact, he ⁵_____ (spend) most of his time online. As for me, I ⁶_____ (give up) yoga and I ⁷_____ (start) dance classes.

What about you? I ⁸_____ (buy) your birthday present, but I ⁹_____ (not buy) a new dress yet for your party! Help!

Love Tina

C Rewrite the Present Perfect sentences or questions using one word from below.

already   ~~ever~~   just   yet (x 2)

1 Have you been to Africa?
   Have you ever been to Africa?

2 Would you like some tea? I've made some.
   _____

3 My mum hasn't met my new girlfriend.
   _____

4 We've done our homework. We did it at school.
   _____

5 Has Tom found a job?
   _____

❶ * Match the sentence beginnings (1–9) with the sentence endings (a–c) so that they have the same meaning as the one above.

I was born here and I still live here now.

1 I have always _b_
2 I have ___
3 I have never ___

a lived here all my life.
b lived here.
c lived anywhere else.

I didn't like pop music when I was young and I don't like it now.

4 I have never ___
5 I have always ___
6 I have ___

a hated pop music all my life.
b liked pop music.
c disliked pop music.

He lived in London when he was a child and still lives there now.

7 He has never ___
8 He has ___
9 He has always ___

a lived in London.
b lived anywhere else.
c lived in London all his life.

❷ ** Complete the sentences so that they have the same meaning as the one above. Use *always* or *never*.

1 I'm not interested in cars now and wasn't interested in them when I was young.
   I ___ *'ve never been* ___ interested in cars.

2 My brother didn't like loud music when he was young and he still doesn't like it.
   My brother _____ loud music.

3 My parents bought this house when they got married and they still live here.
   My parents _____ in the same house.

4 My sister has never had a different hairstyle.
   My sister _____ the same hairstyle.

5 I didn't enjoy computer games when I was young and I still don't.
   I _____ computer games.

6 I have wanted a pet dog all my life.
   I _____ a pet dog.

Sentence Builder *for/since*

3 * Choose the correct words to complete the sentences.

1 I've had the same mobile phone *since/for* about a year.
2 My family has lived in this house *since/for* it was built.
3 I haven't seen my grandparents *since/for* ages.
4 My parents have been married *since/for* 1996.
5 I haven't argued with my mother *since/for* weeks.
6 My best friend has known me *since/for* I started school.

4 ** Complete the sentences so that they have the same meaning as the one above. Use the verb in brackets.

1 I bought a laptop last year.
   I _'ve had a laptop since_ last year. (have)
2 I met my English teacher two years ago.
   I _____ two years. (know)
3 I started at this school in 2012.
   I _____ 2012 (be)
4 My father was born in this city.
   My father _____ he was born. (live)
5 I didn't like rap music when it began. I don't like it now.
   I _____ it began. (like)
6 My mother became interested in French films at university.
   My mother _____ she was at university. (be)

5 *** Write questions with *How long ...* and complete the answers.

1 you / know / your neighbours?
   I / know them / three years
   Q: _How long have you known your neighbours?_
   A: _I have known them for three years._
2 your grandparents / live / at the same address?
   They / live / there / they were married
   Q: _____
   A: _____
3 you / have / your mobile phone?
   I / only have / it / two days
   Q: _____
   A: _____
4 your mother / work / in the same job?
   She / work / in the same job / she / leave school
   Q: _____
   A: _____

6 *** Complete the dialogue with the correct words.

Jane: Granny, how long ¹ _have_ you lived in this house?
Granny: I ² _____ lived here my whole life.
Jane: Wow! What about grandfather?
Granny: He ³ _____ lived here for thirty-five years. I met him at university, so I have known him ⁴ _____ forty years. We got married thirty-five years ago.
Jane: Do you like living in the country?
Granny: Yes, I've ⁵ _____ loved the country. I've ⁶ _____ liked big cities. They're too noisy.
Jane: But when you were young, did you go out much?
Granny: Oh yes, of course. I have always ⁷ _____ interested in music and films. I still love dancing, but I haven't been to a disco ⁸ _____ your mother was born. I haven't had the time or energy!

Grammar Alive Looking back

7 *** Make true sentences for you using the Present Perfect and *always, never, for* or *since*.

1 like school

> I've always liked school.

> I've never liked school.

2 be interested in politics
   _____
3 want to visit Australia
   _____
4 wear second-hand clothes
   _____
5 be good at football
   _____
6 have a boy/girl friend
   _____

1 Complete the note with the verbs below.

want (x 2)   spend   forget (x 2)   make (x 2)   take

Dear Jo

I hope you and your grandma have a nice weekend together.

Don't ¹ _forget_ to tidy your room and ² _____ the rubbish out tonight.

Don't ³ _____ too long on your computer or watching TV, and don't ⁴ _____ too much noise. Your grandmother doesn't like your music. When you make something in the kitchen, don't ⁵ _____ a mess for your grandmother. And if you ⁶ _____ to come back late on Saturday night, don't forget to tell her. If you ⁷ _____ to have more pocket money, ask me, not your grandmother.

See you on Monday, love mum

... and don't ⁸ _____ to do your homework!

2 (1.29) Use the words in brackets to rewrite the <u>underlined</u> phrases. Then listen to check your answers.

1 <u>In my opinion</u>, eleven thirty is a better time. (Personally / think) _Personally, I think_

2 I'm sorry I <u>disagree</u> with you. (not agree)
_____

3 <u>I think</u> eleven thirty is very late. (opinion)
_____

4 <u>In my opinion, it isn't</u> late, mum. (not think)
_____

5 Yeah, <u>I agree with you</u>. (right)
_____

6 <u>In my opinion</u> it's a bit unfair. (really think)
_____

7 I <u>don't agree</u> with that. (disagree)
_____

3 (1.30) Graham and his father are having a conversation. Guess who made the statements (1-6), Graham (G) or his father (F). Then listen and check.

1 I don't think you can do your homework with music on. _F_

2 I'm taking the TV out of your room. ___

3 All my friends multitask. ___

4 You can have the music on – but not so loud and no TV. ___

5 Do you think I can go camping with Sam and Julie in the summer? ___

6 I really think you need one adult with you. ___

4 (1.30) Listen again and complete the opinions.

1 **Father:** I _don't_ think you can do your homework with music on.

   Graham: I'm sorry, I don't _____ with you.

2 **Father:** I'm taking the TV out of your room.

   Graham: I _____ think it's a bit unfair.

3 **Father:** Well, in my _____, you need to think about your homework.

   Graham: Okay, you're _____.

4 **Graham:** Look at my homework. _____ do you think? Is it okay?

   Father: Hmm, yes it's not bad.

5 **Father:** _____ I think TV is for relaxing after you've done your homework.

   Graham: Okay, I agree with _____ about that.

Check Your Progress 5

1 Families Complete the text with the correct words.

I've got two sisters. I get on well [1]_____ both of them but I sometimes argue with Emma, the younger one. We've got a half-brother and a [2]half-_____ from my father's second marriage. Dad lives near our house and we get [3]_____ really well. We have the same tastes [4]_____ music and football teams – but not in fashion! Mum is quite a relaxed person but she [5]_____ angry when we [6]_____ hours on the computer or [7]_____ home late. But we get [8]_____ well most of the time. My grandparents live in a different town and I [9]_____ often see them.

/9

2 Compounds Match the definitions to the correct compounds.

1 to be connected to the Net ___
2 to do different things at the same time ___
3 to get something from the Net (music) ___
4 the first page on a website ___
5 to be disconnected from the Net ___
6 to put something on the Net (photos) ___

a a homepage
b to upload
c to be online
d to multitask
e to download
f to be offline

/6

3 Present Perfect (3) Use the cues to complete sentences in the Present Perfect.

1 How long _____ his computer? (Chris / have)
2 _____ interested in theatre? (Mary / always / be)
3 _____ the colour in my bedroom. (I / never / like)
4 _____ on his own. (Tom / always / live)
5 How long _____ her for? (you / know)
6 _____ living in the city centre. (We / never / enjoy)
7 How long _____ in London? (Sue / live)
8 John _____ to the USA. (never / go)

/8

4 Present Perfect (3) Complete the sentences with *for* or *since*.

1 I've been here _____ 5.30 p.m.
2 They've lived here _____ I was born.
3 I've known her _____ fourteen years.
4 I've had this phone _____ two years.
5 I haven't had this laptop _____ very long.
6 She's been a teacher _____ 2002.

/6

5 Opinions Choose the correct words to complete the sentences.

sorry,   I disagree   I think that's a bit unfair
I really think   In my opinion   What do you think?

A: I've told you to tidy your room 100 times!
B: [1]I'm _____, but I haven't had time.
A: Yes, you have. Saturday afternoon?
B: [2]_____ – I was at the cinema on Saturday.
A: Well, you could do it now – [3]_____
B: [4]_____, now isn't a good time.
A: [5]_____ – now is perfect. Off you go!
B: Oh mum, [6]_____ it's a bit unfair.

/6

TOTAL SCORE   /35

Module Diary

1 Look at the objectives on page 37 in the Students' Book. Choose three and evaluate your learning.

1 Now I can _____
well / quite well / with problems.
2 Now I can _____
well / quite well / with problems.
3 Now I can _____
well / quite well / with problems.

2 Look at your results. What language areas in this module do you need to study more?

Sound Choice 3

1 **1.32** Grammar - regular past endings /t/, /d/ /ɪd/ **Put the verbs in the correct column in the table. Then listen, check and repeat.**

> breathed ~~camped~~ collected downloaded
> logged picked robbed shouted stayed surfed
> touched wanted

/t/	/d/	/ɪd/
camped		

2 **1.33** Grammar - plural endings /z/, /s/ and /ɪz/
Find the word which has a different plural ending sound. Listen, check and repeat.

1 (cousins) forests ships skirts sticks
2 cells clothes glasses jeans stones
3 churches dresses judges nieces shirts

3 **1.34** Consonants - /d/ and /t/ and /s/ and /z/ **Listen and tick the word you hear.**

1 late	✓	laid	☐
2 heart	☐	hard	☐
3 wrote	☐	road	☐
4 sight	☐	side	☐
5 niece	☐	knees	☐
6 close *(adj)*	☐	close *(vb)*	☐
7 bus	☐	buzz	☐
8 force	☐	fours	☐

4 **1.35** Vowels and spelling - the letter 'a' **Listen and repeat the sound and the word. Put the words in the correct column.**

bad along ~~/ɔː/ saw~~ /ɑː/ arm late

/ɔː/	/ɑː/	/a/	/eɪ/	/ə/
1 _saw_	**2** _____	**3** _____	**4** _____	**5** _____
taught	calm	lack	make	arrest
walk	mark	rap	sail	arrive

5 **1.35** Listen and repeat the words from Exercise 4.

6 **1.36** Expressions **Listen and repeat.**

1 It's really imaginative.
2 I'm afraid of heights.
3 I'm interested in reading classics.
4 My mum picked me up yesterday.
5 My brother can't stand my music.
6 What do you upload to your homepage?
7 I've always been interested in sport.
8 My sister always spends too long in the bathroom.

7 **1.37** Difficult words - word stress
Match the words with the correct stress patterns. Then listen, check and repeat.

1 ■■ _ _f_		**a** certificate
2 ▪■ ___		**b** comfortable
3 ■▪▪ ___		**c** exciting
4 ▪■▪ ___		**d** explain
5 ▪■▪▪ ___		**e** generation
6 ▪▪■▪ ___		**f** island

TOPIC TALK - VOCABULARY

1 What are the instruments?

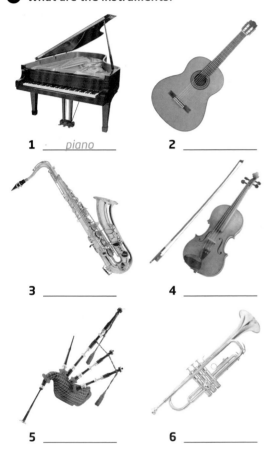

1 _piano_   2 _____

3 _____   4 _____

5 _____   6 _____

2 Complete the sentences with the words below.

rap   chilling out   cello   ~~country and western~~
reggae   keyboards

1 My cousin lives in America and she loves _country and western_ music.
2 My friend plays the _____ - she's so small though and it's so big!
3 I love _____ to classical music.
4 I prefer the sound of a real piano to _____ .
5 My mum can't stand _____ music, she says they talk too quickly and she can't understand.
6 Did you know that _____ music started in Jamaica?

3 Complete the sentences with the correct form of the words in brackets.

1 I can't stand _listening_ (listen) to the blues. It's music for old people!
2 My friends are into pop music, but I just love _____ (listen) to classical music.
3 I'd like _____ (play) the saxophone, but I think it's quite difficult.
4 I can _____ (play) the guitar quite well, so I'm going to join a band.
5 I don't usually listen to music at home, but I like _____ (dance) to music at discos.

4 Order the words in the sentences.

1 into / soul / not / I'm / really
   I'm not really into soul.
2 about / I'm / Take That / crazy
   _____
3 just / to / folk / My / listening / music / father / loves
   _____
4 stand / I / techno / can't
   _____
5 mother / play / My / clarinet / the / can
   _____
6 good / got / I / voice / haven't / singing / a
   _____

5 Complete the text with the correct words below.

about   can't   into   just   listening   play   really
stand   ~~to~~   voice

The worst thing about family holidays is the car journey. Nobody can agree on the music! My dad loves listening ¹ _to_ jazz or very old blues music. He ² _____ stand heavy metal, punk or techno. My sister is really ³ _____ hip hop and rap – she's crazy ⁴ _____ Snoop Dogg – but my mother doesn't think that's 'real music'. Mum can ⁵ _____ the flute and she likes ⁶ _____ to classical music. I'm not ⁷ _____ into pop or classical but I ⁸ _____ love listening to old indie bands like The Smiths. I think Morrissey has got an amazing singing ⁹ _____ . Mum can't ¹⁰ _____ the arguments and says she's going to get everybody an MP3 player. Well I think we can all agree on that!

16 GRAMMAR
have to/not have to, can/can't

REMEMBER

Complete exercises A–D before you start this lesson.

A Use the cues to write sentences with *can* and *can't*.

1 I / Russian / not German (speak)
   I can speak Russian but I can't speak German.

2 I / the piano / not guitar (play)
   _____

3 I / a bike / not a scooter (ride)
   _____

4 I / pasta / not cakes (make)
   _____

B Use the cues to write questions with *can*. Then write the short answers.

1 you / sing?
   Can you sing? Yes, I can./No, I can't.

2 you / dance?
   _____

3 your parents / ski?
   _____

4 your mother / read music?
   _____

5 you / remember your first day at school?
   _____

C Complete the sentences with *have to* (✔) or *don't have to* (✗) and the verb in brackets.

1 You _have to drive_ on the left. (✔ drive)

2 You _____ school when you are five.
   (✔ start)

3 You _____ school when you're sixteen.
   (✗ leave)

4 You _____ a helmet on a motorbike.
   (✔ wear)

5 You _____ an ID card. (✗ carry)

6 You _____ a passport to travel abroad.
   (✔ get)

D Use the cues to write questions with *have to*.

1 you / get up before 7 a.m.?
   Do you have to get up before 7 a.m.?

2 you / take any English exams this year?
   _____

3 father / travel for his job?
   _____

4 mother / drive to work?
   _____

❶ * Choose the correct words to complete the sentences.

1 A singer *has to*/can know the lyrics to each song.
2 Mrs Smith says you *can/don't have to* practise the piano in the music room at school if you want to.
3 A new band *can't/has to* practise a lot.
4 A drummer *has to/doesn't have to* be a good dancer.
5 A keyboard player usually *can/has to* learn to read music.
6 Mr Bond says you *can't/don't have to* sing in maths class – it disturbs other students.

❷ ** Complete the sentences with can/*can't* or *have to/don't have to*.

1 This is a big secret. You __*can't*__ tell anyone okay?
2 You _____ come in. I'm ready!
3 We've got lots of time. We _____ hurry.
4 Come on, come on! We _____ be late.
5 You _____ practise everyday if you want to be good at the piano.
6 She's not very good at maths, so she _____ study very hard.

❸ ** Complete the text with can/*can't*, have to/*don't have to* and the correct form of the verbs below.

Guitar Lessons – For All Levels

You ¹___ *don't have to* ___ play the guitar already.

£15 per lesson – you ²_____ pay when you arrive. You can pay at the end.

You ³_____ bring your own music, or you can borrow mine.

You ⁴_____ have your own guitar – you ⁵_____ borrow a guitar.

⁶_____ you let me know by Friday? – Sign up here.

4 *** Complete the dialogue with the correct form of the verbs in brackets.

Rob: I've never played this game before. What
¹ *do we have to do* (we / do)?

Tina: Well, first we need two teams. Then each team
² _____ (write) some titles on pieces of paper. For example, you can use film titles or book titles.

Rob: I see. ³_____ I _____ (write) song titles?

Tina: Yes, you can. After that, one person from our team chooses a piece of paper from your team. He reads the title silently. Then he ⁴_____ (mime) the title and we ⁵_____ (guess) what it is.

Rob: ⁶_____ he _____ (speak)?

Tina: No, he can't. He ⁷_____ (make) any noise at all. He just has to act.

Rob: Oh dear, I'm not very good at acting.

Tina: Don't worry, you ⁸_____ (be) good. In fact, it's much more fun if you're really bad at acting … like me.

Grammar Alive Complaining

5 * Complete the dialogue with *can't, have to* and *don't have to.*

A: I'm bored.

B: Why don't you watch TV?

A: I ¹ *can't* the TV is broken … and I'm hungry.

B: Well, why don't you make a sandwich?

A: Do I ²_____? Why don't you make it?

B: No, I'm not hungry and anyway I ³_____ (finish) this homework.

A: You ⁴_____ (not / finish) it today. Oh … I've got a headache.

B: Do ⁵_____ (you) complain all the time - why don't you go for a walk?

A: I ⁶_____ … I'm too tired.

6 ** Read these teenage complaints and <u>underline</u> the correct form. Then add two complaints of your own using *can* and *have to.*

1 I *can/can't* go online after 9 p.m. My parents say I *have to/don't have to* switch the computer off for an hour before I go to bed.

2 I *have to/don't have to* be home by 11 p.m. When I'm more than fifteen minutes late, I *can/can't* go out for a whole week.

3 At the school I go to we *can/can't* wear trainers so I *have to/don't have to* wear these horrible black shoes.

4 I *have to/don't have to* share a bedroom with my little sister so I *can/can't* read when I go to bed.

5

6

1 **1.38** Listen to four people at the Glastonbury Festival. Match them with the things they like.

Kelly   Simon   Paula   Nick

1 Thom Yorke of Radiohead _Simon_
2 DJs and the Dance Village _____
3 the sunny weather _____
4 the festival at night _____
5 Kylie Minogue _____
6 the interesting people _____
7 Shakira _____
8 the pizza. _____

2 **1.38** Listen again. Are the sentences true (T) or false (F)?

1 It's always hot and sunny at Glastonbury. ___
2 Kelly's favourite singers include Kate Nash. ___
3 Thom Yorke of Radiohead is singing on the main stage. ___
4 Only young people go to Glastonbury. ___
5 You can go shopping all night if you want. ___
6 Glastonbury is an electronic music festival. ___
7 You can only watch bands at Glastonbury. ___

Vocabulary

3 Match the words (1-9) with their meanings (a-i).

1 big names _e_   a people who watch the bands
2 dance tent ___   b place where bands perform
3 pop, indie, blues ___ c traditional music
4 stage ___   d too many people
5 audience ___   e famous musicians
6 queues ___   f relax
7 chill out ___   g types of music
8 world music ___   h lines of people
9 crowded ___   i place to dance

Sentence Builder *Verbs + adjectives*

4 Complete the text with the words below.

feel (x 2)   looks   sounds (x 2)

1 Snoop Dog _looks_ cool in his white t-shirt and trousers.
2 The music on the main stage _____ great.
3 I _____ really hot - I have to drink a lot of water.
4 My friend _____ tired in the morning.
5 There are 177,000 people here, but it doesn't _____ crowded.
6 Shakira _____ amazing - I love her music.

Word Builder Multi-part verbs (2)

5 Choose the correct words to complete the text.

I like different kinds of music at different times of the day. I ¹turn on/turn down my music when I wake up in the morning, and listen to reggae. I ²turn the volume up/turn the volume down and dance around my bedroom. Reggae makes me feel happy in the morning. When I'm on the bus to school, I ³turn my MP3 player off/turn my MP3 player on and I listen to Metallica. I ⁴turn the volume down/turn the volume up really loud. In the evening, I play electronic music with my friends. My parents often get angry and so we ⁵turn it down/turn it on for a few minutes, and then we ⁶turn it up/turn it off again. I listen to music on the radio when I go to bed. Sometimes I fall asleep and my mother has to ⁷turn it off/turn it up in the middle of the night.

GRAMMAR
LESSON 18
may, must and *must not*

1 * Choose the correct words to complete the sentences.

1 In a park, you *must/mustn't* walk on the grass.
2 On a bus, you *must/mustn't* talk to the driver.
3 In a library, students *may/mustn't* borrow up to six books.
4 In an exam, students *must/mustn't* answer all the questions.
5 To drive a car, students *may/must* have a licence.
6 In a hotel, guests *may/must* use the pool between 4 p.m. and 10 p.m.

2 ** Rewrite each music teacher's instruction with *must* or *mustn't*.

1 Practise your solo!
   → _____ *You must practise your solo.* _____
2 Listen to me!
   → _____
3 Don't play so loud!
   → _____
4 Keep in time!
   → _____
5 Stop talking!
   → _____
6 Don't forget your music next time!
   → _____

3 *** Read the college rules and complete the sentences using *must, may* or *mustn't*.

Music college rules

ALLOWED:

Wear jeans to lessons
Stay up until midnight
Have parties on Saturdays
Play whatever kind of music you like

NECESSARY:

Clean your instruments once a week
Get at least sixty-five percent in exams
Be back at college by 6 p.m.

NOT ALLOWED:

Leave the school without telling a teacher
Miss lessons
Listen to MP3 players after 10 p.m.

Students ...
1 ___ *must* ___ get at least sixty-five percent in exams.
2 _____ after 10 p.m.
3 _____ they like.
4 _____ to lessons.
5 _____ once a week.
6 _____ lessons.
7 _____ a teacher.
8 _____ midnight.
9 _____ on Saturdays.
10 _____ by 6 p.m.

4 *** Complete the sentences for each sign. Use *may, must, mustn't* and the verbs below.

download   like   ~~make~~   pay   stand up   take

1
No noise! We're practising!
You *mustn't make a noise*. We're practising.

2
Free music on our website!
You _____ from our website and you don't have to pay for it.

3
Concert tonight. Tickets £5.
You _____ for a ticket to the concert.

4
Singer wanted for heavy metal band.
You _____ heavy metal if you want to be our singer.

5
PHOTOS ALLOWED FOR PERSONAL USE ONLY.
You _____ photos but only for personal use.

6
No dancing! People standing up during the concert will be asked to leave.
You _____ during the concert.

Workshop 3

Writing

1 Match the parts of the letter (a-h) with the formal expressions (1-8)

1 I totally disagree with the reviewer. _e_
2 In my opinion ___
3 Yours faithfully ___
4 I found this article very disappointing ___
5 In conclusion ___
6 I am writing about ___
7 Dear editor ___
8 According to the reviewer ___

---

a Hi there

b I want to tell you about your review of Miley Cyrus's new album in your magazine last week. Although I am a regular reader of your magazine, **c** for me it was a really bad article.

The reviewer thinks that the album is exciting and full of catchy tracks. **d** The reviewer says the singer has a strong voice, the music is imaginative and the lyrics are interesting.

I am sorry but **e** the reviewer's wrong. I think that Miley Cyrus is a talented actor but she does not have a strong voice. The music is not very original. The songs are repetitive and similar to her earlier albums. The lyrics are boring and have nothing to do with real life. **f** I think, there is only one catchy track, and that's the last one.

g Anyway, I think the review is poor.

h All the best,

Miley Cyrus

Matt Desmond

---

2 Write a letter to a magazine in reply to a review about the new Red Box album. Write a letter of 100-120 words, disagreeing with the review.

RED BOX

A few of the songs are catchy but I'm afraid Grace, the singer, is not very talented. She has a weak voice, and the singing is poor. The lyrics are terrible, and the guitar playing is repetitive and boring. The drums and keyboard are disappointing, too.

Paragraph 1 – Your reasons for writing
Paragraph 2 – The magazine reviewer's opinion
Paragraph 3 – Reasons why you disagree
Paragraph 4 – Your conclusion

Speaking

1 **1.39** Listen to the conversation between Jane and Rob. Circle Jane's opinion (1-4). Put a tick ✔ when Rob agrees and a cross ✘ when he disagrees.

1 I like/I don't like Lady Gaga. __✘__
2 I'm really into/I'm not really into hip hop. _____
3 I really like/I really don't like Alicia Keys. _____
4 I'm/I'm not a heavy metal person. _____

2 **1.39** Match Rob's responses below with opinions 1-4 in Exercise 1. Listen again and check.

Me too _3_   I am ___   I don't ___   Me neither ___

3 Use the cues in brackets to write replies to these sentences.

1 I'm really into country and western. _Me too._ (agree)
2 I'm not a techno person. _____ (agree)
3 I don't like Eminem. _____ (disagree)
4 I really like indie music. _____ (disagree)
5 I'm not into pop. _____ (agree)
6 I like all kinds of music. _____ (agree)

Check Your Progress 6

1 Music **Complete the sentences with the correct word.**

1 Patrick isn't really _____ soul.
2 Lara is _____ into hip hop.
3 Joe just loves _____ to country and western.
4 Steph is crazy _____ The Killers.
5 Joby _____ stand jazz.
6 Zoe's got a really good singing _____.
7 I'd like to _____ the piano.
8 I love relaxing to _____ music.

/8

2 *can/can't/have to/not have to* **Choose the correct words to complete the text.**

I play the drums in a heavy metal band. We ¹*can't/ don't have to* practise during the week because we all go to different schools, so we ²*have to/don't have to* meet up at the weekend. We decided to practise at my house so I ³*don't have to/can't* carry the drums anywhere. We ⁴*can/can't* play in the house because we're too loud. So we ⁵*can't/have to* practise in the garage at the bottom of the garden. It's a bit cold sometimes but at least we ⁶*have to/can* make a noise. We ⁷*can/ have to* practise all day if we want to! We ⁸*don't have to/can* worry about the noise!

/8

3 Verbs + adjectives **Complete the sentences with the correct form of** *feel, look* **or** *sound*.

1 I've listened to their second album. It _____ just like the first one.
2 I always _____ positive when I'm listening to reggae music.
3 She _____ amazing on stage. It's a shame she can't sing.
4 I found a 1980s photo of U2. They _____ so young.
5 My CDs _____ so much better on my new music system.
6 We _____ happy when we dance to pop music.

/6

4 Multi-part verbs (2) **Complete the sentences with the correct words.**

1 Turn the volume _____, I can't hear what they are saying!
2 Turn the radio _____, I want to listen to the weather forecast.
3 Turn your mobile _____, we're in a church!
4 Turn the computer _____, we're trying to save electricity.
5 Turn that music _____, it's too loud and it sounds awful!

/5

5 *may, must* and *mustn't* **Complete each sentence with** *must, mustn't* **or** *may*.

1 You _____ go in now - the head teacher is ready to see you.
2 You _____ go in now - there is an exam in progress.
3 You _____ swim here - it's very dangerous.
4 You _____ swim here - but be very careful.
5 _____ we go now? - have you finished asking us questions?
6 _____ we go now? - I'm having such a good time.
7 You _____ drive on the left - you're in England!
8 You _____ drive on the left - you're in Poland!

/8
TOTAL SCORE /35

Module Diary

1 **Look at the objectives on page 45 in the Students' Book. Choose three and evaluate your learning.**

1 Now I can _____
well / quite well / with problems.
2 Now I can _____
well / quite well / with problems.
3 Now I can _____
well / quite well / with problems.

2 **Look at your results. What language areas in this module do you need to study more?**

Exam Choice 3

Reading

1 Read the text and choose the best answers to the questions.

1 What is the author of the article trying to do?
 a give practical information about travel and cost
 b recommend the festival
 c review the music
 d describe his/her experiences

2 Why is The Underage Festival different from other festivals?
 a It's for music-lovers.
 b It's for teenagers and adults.
 c It's just for teenagers.
 d It's just for adults.

3 Can a thirteen-year-old teenager go to The Underage Festival?
 a Yes, they can.
 b No, they can't.
 c Yes, they can go to the festival with an adult.
 d Yes, they can go to the festival with a teenager between fourteen and eighteen.

4 Where can parents find information about the festival?
 a outside the gate
 b from Sam Kilcoyne, the organiser
 c from their teenage children
 d on the festival website

5 Which of the following can't you have at the Underage Festival?
 a a Chinese meal
 b a pizza
 c a burger and chips
 d your own food

6 Why is it difficult to choose which band to watch?
 a There are six stages.
 b The bands only play for a short time.
 c There's a big variety of music.
 d The music is fantastic.

The Underage Festival

Are you a music-lover between the ages of fourteen and eighteen? Would you like to go to a festival with friends of the same age as you? Then this music festival is for you! For most music festivals you have to be eighteen before you can go without an adult, but the Underage Festival is different. You must be between fourteen and eighteen.

The Underage Festival is a day of music and fun for teenagers. It takes place in Victoria Park, London, in August. It's a one-day festival – it starts at 11.30 a.m. and the music goes on until 8 p.m.

Sam Kilcoyne is the main organiser of the festival. He started The Underage Festival in 2007 when he was only fifteen-years-old. It's a small festival with 10,000 people but the best thing about it is that there are no adults! Parents can wait for their children outside the gate, but they can't come in to the festival.

But parents don't need to worry! The organisation is great and it's a safe and peaceful festival. You can't bring food or drink into the festival, but there are lots of restaurant tents with a variety of food and drink – from pizzas to burgers and Chinese to Mexican. We recommend the pizza tent. On the festival website, there's a page for parents with all the information they need.

There's a big variety of music, everything from indie to hip hop, electronic to heavy metal. There's even a silent disco where everyone wears headphones.

There are six stages. The main stage is outside and the other five are in huge tents. Sometimes, it feels a little crowded in the tents, but the big names usually play on the main stage. Sometimes it's difficult to choose which band to watch because they only play for thirty minutes. But in general, the music is fantastic and the teenagers are happy.

Listening

2 **1.40** Listen to DJ Rocky's answers (a-f) and match them with the questions (1-6). There is one extra question.

1 What kind of music do you listen to to relax? ___
2 How many hours do you work every day? ___
3 What's your favourite festival? ___
4 How did you start being a DJ? ___
5 How often do you go to festivals? ___
6 Do you enjoy your work? ___

3 **1.40** Listen again. Are the sentences true (T) or false (F)?.

1 DJ Rocky wanted to be a music teacher. ___
2 He only plays in clubs in Europe. ___
3 DJ Rocky loves small festivals. ___
4 He's got young children so his job is difficult. ___
5 He listens to classical music to relax. ___

Speaking

4 Complete the dialogue with the words below.

disagree   do   don't   neither   opinion   right   too   think

Tim: I think it's really cool to be in a band.
Becky: I ¹_____. I think it's really hard work. You have to practise and rehearse all the time. I don't ²_____ you have time for going out.
Tim: I ³_____ with that. When you're in a band you go out all the time. I want to start a band.
Becky: But you have to be talented to be in a band. In my ⁴_____, you're not a talented musician.
Tim: You're ⁵_____, but I can learn.
Becky: What do you want to play?
Tim: I really like the guitar but I don't know how to play it.
Becky: I ⁶_____. And I've got a good singing voice, too.
Tim: Really? Great - you can be in my band. What sort of music do you like?
Becky: I like lots of different kinds of music.
Tim: Me ⁷_____.
Becky: But I'm not really into hip hop or rap.
Tim: Me ⁸_____. I like indie and dance music.
Becky: So when do we start rehearsing then?

5 **1.41** Listen and check your answers to Exercise 4.

Exam Choice 3

Use of English

6 **Choose the correct answers.**

I come from a very musical family and I've ¹_____ been interested in music. My mum's second husband, my ²_____ taught me how to play the guitar when I was ten years old. Now, I'm crazy ³_____ heavy metal. Mum and dad hate my long, ⁴_____ hair and strange clothes but I'm in a band so I need to look cool!

Actually, my mum and dad are very easy-going. ⁵_____ they don't like my music, they are happy that I am in a band and enjoying myself. I still live at home so I ⁶_____ to do what they tell me sometimes. I can't ⁷_____ my room in a mess!

The band I'm in has written a few songs. We haven't got any CDs but we've ⁸_____ some of our songs to our website. People ⁹_____ pay to download them. My parents think we're mad to give away our music for nothing but, in my ¹⁰_____ it's a good way to become popular.

1 a never
  b always
  c already
  d ever

2 a half-father
  b stepfather
  c father-in-law
  d grandfather

3 a on
  b for
  c with
  d about

4 a baggy
  b pierced
  c tight
  d dyed

5 a However
  b But
  c Although
  d Personally

6 a must
  b have
  c may
  d can

7 a leave
  b make
  c get
  d put

8 a turned up
  b multitasked
  c uploaded
  d downloaded

9 a mustn't
  b can't
  c don't have to
  d may

10 a opinion
  b thought
  c agree
  d disagree

Writing

7 **Match the sentence beginnings (1-5) with the sentence endings (a-e).**

1 The music sounds great, ___
2 There are 100,000 people here. ___
3 Although the singer looks really cool, ___
4 He has been in the band for two years, ___
5 I like many different kinds of music. ___

a her voice is terrible.
b but the festival is too crowded.
c However, it doesn't feel crowded.
d However, I'm not into hip hop or rap.
e but this year he's recording a solo album.

8 **Read the music blog entry and complete the reply with the linkers below.**

but   however   although

> 'I love Rihanna. She's so beautiful, and I think she's the best female singer in the world.'

I really like Rihanna, ¹_____ I don't think she's the best singer in the world. ²_____ I haven't been to one of her concerts, I have watched her on television. She looks great, and her clothes are very imaginative and interesting. ³_____ I think Beyoncé is more beautiful than Rihanna.

9 **Read the music blog entry and write your own reply.**

> 'There are some good American bands, but the best bands in the world are British. For example, the Arctic Monkeys are brilliant and their lyrics are better than any other bands.'

TOPIC TALK – VOCABULARY

1 Match the pictures with the descriptions.

1

2

3

4

5

6

a Earl has earache. _3_
b Fiona feels faint. ___
c Don has diarrhoea. ___
d Tod has a temperature. ___
e Heather has hayfever. ___
f Tina has toothache. ___

2 Complete the questions with *a, an* or (-).

1 Have you ever had ___a___ serious illness?
2 Did you have _____ flu last year?
3 Do you ever have _____ hayfever?
4 When was the last time you had _____ cold?
5 Have you ever had _____ accident at school?
6 How many times have you been to _____ hospital?

3 Choose the correct words to complete the sentences.

1 Tess has a terrible cough and a sore throat, I think she may have *a cold*/*hayfever*.
2 I feel really tired. I have a sore throat and a high temperature. I think I may have *flu/diarrhoea*.
3 Toby and his friends all have a temperature and feel very faint. I think they need to sunbathe a lot *more/less*.
4 Sandra feels tired and weak all the time. She needs to sleep more and *do/make* more exercise.
5 Len has never had a bad illness but he occasionally *has/feels* depressed.

4 Complete the sentences with *more* or *less* in the correct place.

1 People need to do _more_ exercise.
2 People really need to eat fruit.
3 People need to watch TV.
4 People really need to eat junk food.
5 People need to sunbathe.

5 Complete the text with the correct words.

Harry is really healthy. He eats fruit and vegetables every day and he never eats junk ¹ _food_. He's stopped smoking so he never has ² _____ cough or a sore ³ _____. He's never ⁴ _____ to hospital, and he's never had ⁵ _____ accident.

Ursula is really unhealthy. She eats junk food and chocolate every day, and she smokes. She often ⁶ _____ toothache and stomachache. She sometimes has a headache and ⁷ _____ faint. I think it's because she never goes outside. She needs to ⁸ _____ more exercise. She also needs ⁹ _____ eat more fruit and vegetables and she ¹⁰ _____ needs to stop smoking.

1 Read the article and choose the best summary.

a The sun is bad for your skin.

b The sun is good for your skin but in summer you must use protection.

c The sun is bad for people with fair skin, but fine for people with dark skin.

SUMMER SKIN CARE – FACT OR FICTION?

In summer everybody needs to be careful with the sun. Do you know how to spend time in the sun without burning or damaging your skin? Read the ten rules below and find out which are FACT and which are FICTION.

1 **Always wear a baseball cap. It protects you from the sun and looks cool, too.** FICTION You need to wear a hat, but choose your hat carefully. Baseball caps protect your eyes, but they don't protect your ears or your neck. Use a proper sun hat.

2 **Use sun cream. You need to put it on at least twenty minutes before you go out.** FACT Sun cream starts to work twenty minutes after you put it on.

3 **Put sun cream around your eyes and on your eyelids to protect them from the sun.** FICTION Sun cream hurts the eyes. Wear sunglasses instead.

4 **You only need a little sun cream. Too much sun cream is bad for your skin.** FICTION You need to use a lot of sun cream. The sun dries out your skin. Sun cream moisturises and protects it.

5 **Put more sun cream on every two hours.** FACT You need to put sun cream on regularly, especially when you're swimming.

6 **You need to use sun cream even on a cloudy day in summer.** FACT The sun can damage your skin even on a cloudy day.

7 **On a hot sunny day, wear light-coloured clothes – white or yellow are best.** FICTION Light coloured clothes don't protect you from the sun. The best solution is to wear baggy clothes in dark colours.

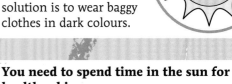

8 **You need to spend time in the sun for healthy skin.** FACT You need to spend time in the sun to get enough vitamin D for healthy skin and bones, but don't forget to use sun cream. Without sun cream you have a bigger risk of skin cancer.

9 **You need to spend a lot of money to get a good sun cream.** FICTION There are many different brands of sun cream. Find the one that is best for you. Expensive ones are not always better than cheap ones. Use a sun cream labelled SPF30+ and it should give you the same protection as one that is more expensive.

10 **In summer, people with dark skin can also get burnt.** FACT People with fair skin and blonde or red hair need to be extra careful and use a high factor sun cream. People with dark skin can stay in the sun longer than people with fair skin, but they do need to protect their skin from the sun, too.

2 **Choose the best answer to the questions.**

1 What are the right clothes to protect your skin from the sun?
  a a baseball hat and light coloured clothes
  b a baseball hat and dark coloured clothes
  c a sun hat and light coloured clothes
  d a sun hat and dark coloured clothes

2 Where shouldn't you put sun cream on your body?
  a on your ears and neck
  b around your eyes and eyelids
  c on dry skin
  d on darker skin

3 What is the right way to use sun cream?
  a Use a little and often.
  b Use a lot, two or three times a day.
  c Use a lot every two hours.
  d Use a little every two hours.

4 Why is it important to spend time in the sun?
  a You drink more water.
  b It improves dry skin.
  c It's a chance to wear cool sunglasses.
  d It helps keep your skin and bones healthy.

5 What kind of sun cream is best?
  a an expensive one
  b a cheap one
  c a cream labelled SPF30+
  d a moisturising one

Word Builder Confusing words

3 **Choose the correct word to complete the sentences.**

1 In the past, people didn't know about the dangers of smoking. *Now*/*Actually* we know that it causes cancer.

2 A year ago I wasn't very fit, but *now/actually* I go running every day. *Now/Actually* I'm training for a marathon.

3 I love eating sweets but my dentist says they *damage/hurt* my teeth. I hate going to the dentist because it really *damages/hurts* a lot.

4 I had a lovely *meal/food* in an Italian restaurant yesterday. I had a pizza but it was too *great/big* and I couldn't finish it.

5 I'm allergic to the sun so I *wear/use* a hat and sunglasses all the time. I also *wear/use* a special high factor sun cream.

Writing

4 **Read the instructions for making lemonade and put the pictures in the correct order.**

The perfect lemonade recipe

1 [b] _First_ take one cup of sugar and put it in one cup of hot water.

2 ☐ _____ squeeze four to six lemons and then add the lemon juice to the sugar water.

3 ☐ _____ mix the lemon juice and sugar water with three to four cups of cold water.

Too sweet?

4 ☐ _____ put less sugar and more lemon juice.

5 **Complete the instructions in Exercise 4 with the linkers below.**

Finally   Then   Next time   ~~First~~

GRAMMAR
will, may and *be going to*

REMEMBER

Complete exercises A–C before you start this lesson.

A Complete the sentences with *will* (✔) or *won't* (✗) and the verb in brackets.

Fifty years from now …
1 People _will live_ longer. (✔ live)
2 Health care _____ free anywhere in the world. (✗ be)
3 Children _____ a lot more allergies like hay fever. (✔ get)
4 Malaria _____ in Europe. (✔ exist)
5 Teenagers _____ as much sport. (✗ do)

B Complete each of the health resolutions with the correct form of *going to*.

New Year's health resolutions
1 ✔ Tom _is going to_ stop eating chocolate.
2 ✗ My friends _aren't going to_ make so many mobile phone calls.
3 ✔ Mum and Dad _____ do more exercise.
4 ✔ I _____ eat more fruit and vegetables.
5 ✗ Gemma _____ stay up so late.
6 ✔ Sara _____ cycle to school.
7 ✗ I _____ eat as much fast food.

C Order the words in the questions.
1 getting warmer / the climate / continue / Will ?
   Will the climate continue getting warmer?
2 the gym / Bob and Anna / to / join / going / Are ?
   _____
3 Will / this evening / your mum / at home / be ?
   _____
4 live / on the moon / people / Will / ever ?
   _____
5 to / to school / today / going / you / Are / walk ?
   _____

1 * Order the words in the sentences predicting your future health and well-being.

1 get / probably / married / I'll
   → _I'll probably get married._
2 sure / I'll / I'm / children / have
   → _____
3 in an office / think / work / I / I'll / don't
   → _____
4 put on / I / weight / may
   → _____
5 don't / I'll / think / start / smoking / I
   → _____
6 definitely / eating / junk food / stop / I'll
   → _____
7 I / not / a television / in my home / may / have
   → _____
8 need / glasses / going / soon / I'm / to
   → _____

2 * Complete the predictions for these patients.

1 Jim has broken his arm.
   He may need an operation (may / need an operation)
2 Debbie has a cold. _____
   (will probably / be okay next week)
3 Katy smokes a lot. _____
   (may / get cancer)
4 Giles has really bad toothache.
   _____ (may / need to visit the dentist)
5 Dawn looks very pale and has a stomachache.
   _____ (going to / be sick)
6 Alex eats well and does lots of exercise.
   _____ (will probably live to be 100)

❸ ** Complete the sentences with *will, may* or *be going to* and the correct form of the verbs in brackets.

1 Bye for now. Maybe I __*'ll see*__ you later. (see)
2 Prices are very high in France. You _____ a lot of money for your holiday. (need)
3 There isn't a cloud in the sky, it _____ a beautiful day. (be)
4 I _____ go to the doctors tomorrow - I'll see how I feel in the morning. (go)
5 Perhaps we _____ again one day. (meet)
6 Mum feels tired so she _____ to bed early tonight. (go)
7 Do you think you _____ taller than your dad? (grow)
8 The doctor _____ you antibiotics or he _____ that you don't need them. (give, decide)

❹ *** Complete the dialogue with the phrases below.

I'll be   I'll have to   I'll probably walk   it's going to rain
may agree   may be   may not come   ~~will be~~   will let
won't finish   won't want

Cathy: I don't think Lena ¹ __*will be*__ at the party tonight.
Matt: Why not?
Cathy: She feels cold. She thinks it's flu.
Matt: So, she ² _____ to school tomorrow.
Cathy: Probably not. Does that matter?
Matt: Yes. I'm doing a project with her. We probably ³ _____ it on time now.
Cathy: Don't worry. I'm sure Mr Collins ⁴ _____ you have some extra time. Anyway, don't worry about that now. How are you getting to the party?
Matt: I don't know. It's a nice day, I don't think ⁵ _____ so ⁶ _____. That means ⁷ _____ leave home at about seven o'clock.
Cathy: My dad's taking me. He ⁸ _____ to take you as well.
Matt: Great.
Cathy: He's going to collect me as well but at ten o'clock. You probably ⁹ _____ to leave that early.
Matt: I don't know. The party ¹⁰ _____ boring and I don't want to be too late to bed or ¹¹ _____ tired tomorrow.
Cathy: Is this Matt I'm talking to?!
Matt: Yes, I've changed. I need to be careful about my health.

Grammar Alive Predictions

❺ ** Complete the sentences using a verb from below and the correct form of *be going to, will* or *may*.

be   get (x 2)   leave   live   ~~move~~

1 My parents __*may move*__ to a different house. They aren't sure yet.
2 My sister _____ probably _____ school when she's sixteen. She doesn't like studying.
3 I _____ never _____ in a different country. I love England too much.
4 We _____ flu this year. A lot of people I know have had it.
5 I'm sure you _____ malaria on holiday - you're only going to Brighton.
6 My brother always works very hard in science. He _____ a doctor.

1 Complete the network with a verb from below.

be break get over have hurt take

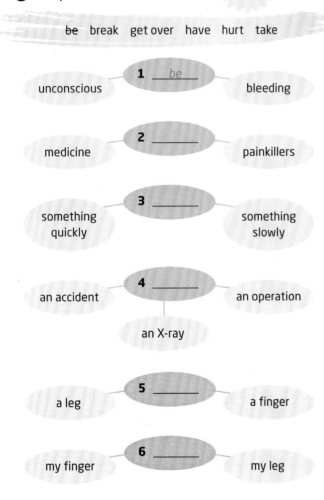

1 __be__ unconscious / bleeding

2 _____ medicine / painkillers

3 _____ something quickly / something slowly

4 _____ an accident / an operation / an X-ray

5 _____ a leg / a finger

6 _____ my finger / my leg

2 Complete the text with the verbs from Exercise 1.

I've never ¹ __had__ an accident, or a serious illness, but my brother isn't so lucky. First, he ² _____ his leg playing football. He didn't ³ _____ it quickly, and in the end he ⁴ _____ two operations. Finally, his leg got better, but six months later he fell off his motorbike. He ⁵ _____ unconscious and his head ⁶ _____ bleeding. He ⁷ _____ lots of X-rays but fortunately he was okay.

3 (2.1) Match (1–10) with (a–j) to complete the dialogue. Listen and check your answers.

1 What's __c__
2 I've got a stomach ___
3 I feel a ___
4 Where ___
5 I've been ___
6 What about ___
7 How long have you ___
8 Have you ___
9 You've got a high ___
10 I'm afraid you've got a ___

a sick twice.
b got any food allergies?
c the problem?
d temperature.
e diarrhoea?
f stomach infection.
g ache.
h does it hurt?
i bit sick.
j had these symptoms?

4 (2.2) Choose the best answers and then listen and check.

Doctor: Hello Simon. What's the ¹ __a__ ?
Simon: I think I've hurt my leg.
Doctor: Right. Do you ² _____ any pain?
Simon: Yes, I have a lot of pain.
Doctor: So where does it ³ _____?
Simon: Here and here.
Doctor: I see. Any vomiting?
Simon: No. I don't ⁴ _____ sick.
Doctor: Good. I'm going to ⁵ _____ your temperature. Hmm. You've got a slight temperature. How long have you had these symptoms?
Simon: Since Saturday. I fell off my bicycle.
Doctor: Ah, well ⁶ _____ afraid you need to have some X-rays.
Simon: Oh, but I'm going camping tomorrow.
Doctor: I'm afraid you're not going anywhere tomorrow. Don't worry, you'll get ⁷ _____ it quickly, but you shouldn't walk on that leg for a while. Take these painkillers four times ⁸ _____ day.

1 a problem   b accident   c illness
2 a are   b have   c got
3 a pain   b feel   c hurt
4 a got   b feel   c be
5 a put   b take   c feel
6 a I'm   b it's   c he's
7 a on   b over   c up
8 a one   b for   c a

Check Your Progress 7

1 Health **Complete the text with the correct words.**

I think I'm quite healthy. I've only been [1]_____ hospital once and that was to have an X-ray. I've never had an [2]_____ or a bad illness. I've [3]_____ flu a couple of times but I soon got over it. I occasionally have [4]_____ headache but that's when I [5]_____ tired because I've stayed up too late. I really need [6]_____ watch less TV and sleep [7]_____. But apart from that I eat well and [8]_____ lots of exercise. I sometimes eat chocolate, but I'm trying to eat [9]_____.

/9

2 Confusing words **Choose the correct words to complete the sentences.**

1 A few weeks ago Jeff was really ill but *now/ actually* he's fine.
2 I take a lot of vitamin pills but *now/actually*, I don't think they do anything.
3 Too much sun can really *hurt/damage* your skin and sunburn can really *hurt/damage*.
4 I love Japanese *meal/food*. The best *meal/food* I've ever had was at a traditional Japanese inn.
5 Hayfever is usually a *great/big* problem for me but this new medicine is *great/big*.

/5

3 *will, may* and *be going to* **Complete the sentences with the correct form of the words in brackets and the words below.**

need   arrive   eat   finish   travel   rain   win   be

1 Tim is at the dentist's. He _____ a bit late. (may)
2 My cousin _____ around the world. (going to)
3 I think people _____ less junk food in the future. (will)
4 It's _____. Look at that blue sky! (not going to)
5 She definitely _____ her book this evening. (won't)
6 Look! Tess _____ _____ the race. (going to)
7 Steve has broken his leg. He _____ an operation. (may)
8 I've got a sore throat. I'm sure I _____ okay next week. (will)

/8

4 Emergencies **Complete the sentences with the correct form of the verbs below.**

be   break   get over   have (x 2)   hurt   take (x 2)

1 The doctor says he's _____ his finger but it's not a serious break.
2 He _____ an accident on his way to school yesterday.
3 Are you _____ any medicine at the moment?
4 Does your leg _____ if I press here?
5 You need to _____ an X-ray as soon as possible.
6 He had flu but he _____ it very quickly.
7 I _____ a painkiller when I have a headache.
8 He _____ bleeding badly when he broke his finger.

/8

5 At the doctors **Complete the dialogue with the correct words.**

A: Hello. What's the [1]_____?
B: I've [2]_____ a temperature.
A: I see. What about a sore [3]_____ or headache?
B: No, I haven't, but I've [4]_____ earache.
A: Oh dear. It sounds like an ear infection. Drink lots of water and [5]_____ these pills four times a day. You'll soon get over it.

/5

TOTAL SCORE   /35

Module Diary

1 Look at the objectives on page 53 in the Students' Book. Choose three and evaluate your learning.

1 Now I can _____
well / quite well / with problems.
2 Now I can _____
well / quite well / with problems.
3 Now I can _____
well / quite well / with problems.

2 Look at your results. What language areas in this module do you need to study more?

Sound Choice 4

Sound Check

Say the words and expressions below.

a you mustn't go/they'll have some (Exercise 1)

b sore mouth, this zoo (Exercise 2)

c bit, beat, cat, cart (Exercises 3 and 4)

d cool, food, should (Exercise 5)

e I'm not really into reggae. (Exercise 6)

f toothache, temperature, moisturising (Exercise 7)

2.3 **Listen and check your answers. Which sounds and expressions did you have problems with? Choose three exercises to do below**

1 **2.4** Grammar - contractions **Listen and tick the phrase you hear.**

1	you must go	✓	you mustn't go ☐
2	he can come ☐		he can't come ☐
3	they'll have some ☐		they have some ☐
4	I'd like it ☐		I like it ☐
5	she doesn't know ☐		she does know ☐
6	we've bought one ☐		we bought one ☐

2 **2.5** Consonants - /ð/, /θ/ or /s/, /z/ **Listen and repeat.**

/θ/ /s/

1 thin skin

2 sore mouth

3 sad thoughts

4 six teeth

/ð/ /z/

5 that disease

6 this zoo

7 those hands

8 these pills

3 **2.6** Vowels - short or long? **Listen and number the words in the order you hear them.**

☐ bit	☐ beat
☐ cat	1 cart
☐ cot	☐ caught
☐ pull	☐ pool

4 **2.6** **Now listen again and repeat the words.**

5 **2.7** Spelling - the letter 'o' **Match the words with the same vowel sound. Then listen, check and repeat.**

1 cool _b_	a folk
2 cough ___	b food
3 crowd ___	c form
4 should ___	d good
5 soap ___	e noise
6 sore ___	f out
7 today ___	g police
8 voice ___	h spot

6 **2.8** Expressions **Listen to the chants and <u>underline</u> the two stressed words or syllables on each line. Then practise repeating the chants.**

A

I'm not <u>really</u> into <u>reggae</u>,

I'm not crazy about rock,

I can't stand heavy metal,

I love techno and hip hop.

B

You shouldn't eat that junk food,

You shouldn't eat that cake,

You should eat more fruit and vegetables,

Drink water, it tastes great!

7 **2.9** Difficult words **First or second syllable stress? Complete the table. Then listen, check and repeat.**

depressed infectious moisturising pneumonia temperature t̶o̶o̶t̶h̶a̶c̶h̶e̶

two syllable words	
■■ *toothache*	■■

three syllable words	
■■■	■■■

four syllable words	
■■■■	■■■■

TOPIC TALK – VOCABULARY

1 Use the picture clues to complete the crossword.

Down

Across

2 Complete the table with the animals from Exercise 1.

Mammals ___hippo___, _____, _____, _____,
_____, _____, _____, _____

Insects _____, _____, _____, _____

Reptiles _____, _____

3 <u>Underline</u> the word that doesn't belong in each group.

1 Green spaces: parks / gardens / <u>traffic</u> / woods
2 Nature reserves: rivers / noise / lakes / wildlife
3 Wild animals: foxes / deer / wolves / dogs
4 Animals which live in water: worms / sharks / jellyfish / toads

4 Complete the text with the words and phrases below.

a In our area   **b** Our climate is probably changing
c the biggest environmental problem
d there are lots of   **e** you can see interesting varieties

I live in a city which was a fishing village. ¹ _a_ there are lots of buildings and there aren't many parks. But although my city is more famous for its shopping centres, ² ___ green spaces. ³ ___, but we still have four seasons – five if you include the rainy season. ⁴ ___ is air pollution because of the traffic. We have a good system of trains, subways and buses, but there are still too many cars. In my city ⁵ ___ of birds and at the zoo you can see endangered species such as pandas and tigers.

REMEMBER

Complete exercises A-C before you start this lesson.

Ⓐ Match the Zero Conditional sentence beginnings (1-6) with the sentence endings (a-f).

1 If you have a very high temperature, _b_
2 If you have really bad toothache, ___
3 If you have flu, ___
4 If you have a headache, ___
5 If you feel faint, ___
6 If you always feel tired and unhealthy, ___

a call a dentist.
b see a doctor.
c change your diet and do some exercise.
d lie down for a while.
e get plenty of rest and drink lots of water.
f take an aspirin.

Ⓑ Complete the Zero Conditional sentences with the correct form of the verbs in brackets.

1 If I _walk_ to school, it _takes_ me about half an hour. (walk / take)
2 I _____ very well if I _____ cola in the evening. (not sleep / drink)
3 If I _____ too much junk food, I _____ sick. (eat / feel)
4 If I _____ swimming, I sometimes _____ earache. (go / get)
5 My mum _____ really grumpy if she _____ enough sleep. (be / not get)
6 Our English teacher _____ angry if we _____ our homework. (get / not do)

Ⓒ Use the cues to write sentences in the Zero Conditional about you.

1 want to relax / listen to classical music
   If I want to relax, I listen to classical music.

2 go to bed late / be tired the next day
   _____

3 get a headache / spend too long on the computer
   _____

4 not do any exercise / feel tired
   _____

5 usually eat chocolate / feel depressed
   _____

❶ * Complete the conditional sentences with *will* and the correct form of the verbs in brackets.

1 If it _rains_ (rain) tomorrow, we _won't go_ (not go) to the zoo.
2 If it _____ (be) a nice day, I _____ (have) lunch in the park.
3 If you _____ (go) camping in the summer, I _____ (go) with you.
4 He _____ (miss) the bus if he _____ (not leave) now.
5 If I _____ (see) John, I _____ (tell) him you called.
6 We _____ (be) late if we _____ (not hurry).
7 If it _____ (not rain) tomorrow, we _____ (go) to the beach.
8 We _____ (be) early if we _____ (leave) now.

❷ ** Match the sentence beginnings (1-6) with the sentence endings (a-f). Write conditional sentences.

Six ways to help save the Planet
1 turn off your TV or computer at night,
2 print on both sides,
3 spend less time in the shower,
4 buy local food,
5 stop drinking bottled water,
6 walk or cycle more,

a waste less water
b reduce plastic pollution
c save electricity.
d reduce traffic pollution (and get fitter)!
e use much less paper
f reduce unnecessary food transportation

1 _c If you turn off your TV or computer at night, you'll save electricity._
2 _____
3 _____
4 _____
5 _____
6 _____

❸ ** Complete the text with the correct form of the verbs in brackets.

Life on Earth is experiencing huge change because of the success of one species – humans. In the last 500 years 844 species have died out. Some scientists believe that in the next few years we ¹_____will lose_____ (lose) another 16,000 species if we ² _don't change_ (not change) our behaviour.

- Habitat loss – If we ³_____ (not stop) destroying the rain forest, many species ⁴_____ (lose) their natural habitat and disappear.
- Hunting – Rare species ⁵_____ (become) extinct if illegal hunting ⁶_____ (continue).
- Over-fishing – Many common fish including tuna and salmon ⁷_____ (not survive) if we ⁸_____ (not control) fishing.
- Pollution – This is the biggest problem and leads to climate change. If the world ⁹_____ (continue) to get hotter, the ice will melt and sea levels will rise.

If we ¹⁰_____ (not act) now, our success may mean disaster for future generations.

Sentence Builder *Time Clauses*

❹ * Rewrite the sentences with the same meaning as the one above.**

1 I'll get home and then I'll text you. (when)
   I'll text you when I get home.

2 It may snow next month and we'll go skiing. (if)
   _____

3 I'll have a shower and then I'll go to school. (before)
   _____

4 He'll be eighteen and then he'll have driving lessons. (when)
   _____

5 She'll read her book and then she'll go to sleep. (before)
   _____

Grammar Alive Negotiating

❺ ** Use the cues to write a conversation between a brother and sister.

Brother:	feed the cat →
Sister:	take the dog for a walk →
Brother:	tidy the kitchen →
Sister:	do the washing up →
Brother:	get me some cola →
Sister:	stop giving me things to do →
Brother:	feed the cat
Brother:	¹_Can you feed the cat?_
Sister:	²_I'll feed the cat if you take the dog for a walk._
Brother:	³_I'll take ..._
Sister:	⁴_____
Brother:	⁵_____
Sister:	⁶_____
Brother:	⁷_____

Listening

1 (2.10) **Listen to a conversation between Grace and Harry. Are the sentences true (T) or false (F)?**

1 Harry went to London for his holidays. _T_
2 Grace went to Australia to visit friends. ___
3 Grace saw box jellyfish in the sea. ___
4 She only went swimming on beaches with lifeguards. ___
5 She didn't see any spiders. ___
6 A huge bird ran after her on the beach. ___

2 (2.10) **Read the postcard from Grace to Emily. Choose the correct answers. Listen again and check your answers.**

I'm having a great time in the ¹a *south* b *west* c *northeast* of Australia. It's really ²a *wet* b *hot* c *cold* here and I'm spending a lot of time ³a *in the park* b *on the beach* c *in the forest*. I had a ⁴a *nasty* b *pleasant* c *funny* experience a couple of days ago. I went for a walk on the beach. I was ⁵a *alone* b *with mum* c *with dad* and I came across ⁶a *a snake* b *a bird* c *a spider*. It was huge, and it ran after me. I ran away but it followed me. I was terrified. Finally I screamed and it ran away into the forest. I hope you're having a good holiday. See you soon, love Grace xx

3 (2.10) **Listen again. Guess the meanings of the words and expressions (1-8).**

1 **tanned**: a tired b brown-skinned c healthy
2 **tropical**: a a very hot, dry climate b a very hot, wet climate c a cold climate
3 **tentacles**: a eyes b teeth c thin arms
4 **lifeguards**: a people who save swimmers in danger b people who sell beds and umbrellas on the beach c people who clean the beach
5 **terrified**: a extremely happy b extremely frightened c extremely tired
6 **aggressive**: a behaving in an angry way b behaving in an amusing way c behaving in a stupid way
7 **chased**: a watched b ran after quickly c walked next to
8 **relieved**: a sad because a happy situation has ended b happy because a funny situation had started c happy because a bad situation has ended

Word Builder Multi-part verbs (3)

4 **Complete the sentences with** *back, across, down* **or** *away*.

1 Emily came __across__ a Cassowary on the beach.
2 She tried to run _____ from it.
3 She couldn't get _____ from it and it chased her into the sea.
4 In the end she decided to fight _____ and she shouted at it.
5 The Cassowary slowed _____ and finally went back to the forest.

Sentence Builder *it*

5 **Read the information about the Cassowary. In which sentences does 'it' refer to The Cassowary?**

The Cassowary lives in the rain forests of Australia and New Guinea. ¹*It* is dark and humid in the forest, and the Cassowary likes to hide away. ²*It* is a large bird – about two metres tall and weighs about sixty kilograms. ³*It* can run nearly fifty kilometres an hour and jump up to 1.5 metres. ⁴*It* is dangerous to disturb a Cassowary as it may run after you and attack you. In fact, according to the Guinness Book of Records, ⁵*it* is the world's most dangerous bird. The Cassowary doesn't fly but ⁶*it* is a good swimmer. The Cassowary is an endangered species and ⁷*it* is illegal to kill them.

LESSON

24 GRAMMAR
all, most, many, some, no/none

❶ * <u>Underline</u> the correct quantifier to complete these facts about birds.

Focus on birds

1 <u>All</u>/None birds use songs to communicate with each other.

2 In *no/most* species of bird it is only the male that sings.

3 *Many/None* of song birds sing from the same place each day.

4 *Some/Some of* birds may repeat their song over 1000 times at one time.

5 *No/Many* birds have ever learned how to speak, they just copy human speech.

6 *Most of/Some* African grey parrots can 'say' up to 1000 words and phrases.

❷ * <u>Underline</u> the word that is *not* possible in each sentence.

1 There are many *trees/<u>pollution</u>/green* spaces in our town.

2 Many *cars/lorries/traffic* drive along here every morning.

3 Climate change causes many *problems/dangers/bad weather*.

4 We've found many *information/stories/articles* about climate change on the internet.

5 I don't like this house. There are many *insects/noise/spiders* here at night.

6 Many *rivers/lakes/water* are polluted.

❸ ** Write sentences about people in the class. Use *none of/no, some, many, most* or *all* in your answers.

1 15% are vegetarian
Some people in the class are vegetarian.

2 85% live in apartments
_____

3 15% speak very good English
_____

4 0% give money to animal charities
_____

5 55% believe in climate change
_____

❹ *** Put the words in bold into the correct place in the sentence.

Many people are terrified of spiders. Why? spiders are not dangerous – even the scary tarantula. It's true that of the larger tarantulas can kill small animals like mice or lizards but did you know that tarantula has ever killed anybody? In fact, only about twenty of the 40,000 species of spider in the world have ever been responsible for a human death. psychologists believe our fear is a learned behaviour – we see somebody standing on a chair shouting 'spider!' and we copy them. scientists think our fears go back to the times when we believed species of insects and spiders carried diseases. Whatever the reasons, it seems that of us want to admit that our fear of spiders – or arachnophobia – is just, well … silly.

many
most

some

no

many

some
all

none

Workshop 4

Writing

1 **Put the questions (1-5) in the correct place (a-e) in the letter below.**

1 Can I bring my laptop?
2 Do I have to go fishing?
3 Can we cook our own food or is there a café?
4 Do I have to do dancing?
5 What is the minimum age to come on your camp?

> Hi there!
>
> I want to know about your Forest Summer Camp.
>
> First, ª __5__? I am fifteen and I'd like to come with my seventeen-year-old brother. Second, ᵇ_____? I'm a vegetarian and I don't eat meat or fish.
>
> <u>Another</u> question is about fishing, ᶜ_____? I'd prefer to do <u>other</u> activities because I don't agree with fishing.
>
> I have also got some practical questions. ᵈ_____? The <u>other</u> thing is my mobile phone. Will I have a signal in the forest?
>
> I'm a bit worried about <u>the other</u> activities. ᵉ_____? I'm not very good at it.
>
> Finally, what time does it finish on Sunday?
>
> Write soon,
>
> All the best
>
> Jack Robbins

2 **Match the <u>underlined</u> words in the letter with the meanings (1-4).**

1 the rest of the __the other__
2 different _____
3 one more _____
4 second _____

3 **Find informal expressions in the letter and replace them with the formal expressions below with the same meaning.**

1 Dear Sir/Madam, __Hi there!__
2 I am writing to ask for information _____
3 I look forward to hearing from you. _____
4 Yours faithfully, _____

Speaking

1 **2.11 Listen to the conversation and choose the correct words to complete the sentences.**

1 I think we should (wait)/to wait for a few minutes.
2 Let's/Why sit down.
3 We will/can eat our sandwiches.
4 Why/What don't we call somebody?
5 Let's to play/play a game.
6 What about/of twenty questions.
7 Let/Let's go back before it gets dark.
8 I think you can/should ask an expert about those mushrooms.

2 **Complete the dialogue with one question word.**

A: Let's do something this weekend.
B: ¹ __What__?
A: We can go camping.
B: ²_____?
A: In the New Forest. We can go with some friends.
B: ³_____?
A: How about Richard and Mike?
B: ⁴_____?
A: Because they've done a lot of camping. Let's call them later.
B: ⁵_____?
A: At five o'clock, after school.

Check Your Progress 8

❶ Environment Complete the sentences with the correct word.

1 Air _____ is worse in big cities.
2 Climate _____ is making the world warmer.
3 Green _____ are places like parks and gardens.
4 Nature _____ help protect wildlife.
5 Environmental _____ are affecting us all.
6 Over- _____ is a problem in all the world's oceans.
7 My _____ animals are deer.
8 Habitat _____ is a big problem for many animals.

/8

❷ Future Conditional Complete the sentences with *will* and the correct form of the verbs in brackets.

1 If you _____ (leave) the dog alone, it _____ (not bite) you.
2 I _____ (take) the dog for a walk if you _____ (feed) the cat.
3 If he _____ (not arrive) soon, we _____ (start) without him.
4 I _____ (be) very angry if he _____ (lose) my MP3 player.
5 What _____ (you do) if you _____ (not pass) your exams?
6 If we _____ (go) by bus, we _____ (not be) late.

/6

❸ Multi-part verbs (3) Replacing the <u>underlined</u> phrases with the correct form of the multi-part verbs in the box.

come across   fight back   get away   run away
slow down   stay away from

1 <u>Go fast in the opposite direction</u> from alligators – they can't go very far on land.
2 If you meet a tiger, stand still and prepare to <u>be aggressive, too</u>.
3 <u>Don't go near</u> bears. They don't go near humans.
4 Be extremely careful if you <u>meet</u> a mother bear with cubs by chance.
5 Bears run fast and climb trees so it's really difficult to <u>escape</u> from them.
6 If you run through bushes you can make killer bees <u>move more slowly</u>.

/6

❹ *it* Add *it* to the text where necessary. (There are eight missing)

My cousin has a pet snake and he keeps in a cage. I think is bad to keep animals in cages, but he looks after very well, so I suppose it's happy. was quite small when he first got, but now it's grown to about a metre long. One day I went to his house and he said 'That's strange. I shut the door of the cage last night, but was open this morning and the snake isn't there!' As you can imagine, was very frightening to think that this big snake was free, and probably somewhere in the house. I left very quickly, and didn't return to my cousin's house until he'd found.

/8

❺ *all, most, many, some, no, none* Choose the correct words to complete the sentences.

1 It's been so hot – there is *no/none* water left in our lake.
2 *Some/None* insects are in danger of extinction.
3 *No/None of* the animals in the zoo are happy.
4 *All/Many* the students in my class are vegetarian.
5 *All/Most* people are worried about climate change.
6 There are *many/no* species of birds in my garden.
7 *Most/Many* of the wildlife is protected.

/7

TOTAL SCORE /35

Module Diary

❶ Look at the objectives on page 61 in the Students' Book. Choose three and evaluate your learning.

1 Now I can _____
   well / quite well / with problems.
2 Now I can _____
   well / quite well / with problems.
3 Now I can _____
   well / quite well / with problems.

❷ Look at your results. What language areas in this module do you need to study more?

Exam Choice 4

Reading

1 Match the numbers (1-8) with the words (a-h).

1	100,000,000 ___	**a**	one hundred
2	90 ___	**b**	fourteen percent
3	100 ___	**c**	eighty
4	3,500 ___	**d**	one hundred million
5	80 ___	**e**	fifty percent
6	130 ___	**f**	ninety
7	14% ___	**g**	one hundred and thirty
8	50% ___	**h**	three thousand five hundred

2 Read the text and complete the information using the numbers in Exercise 1.

1 _____ Monarch butterflies travel to Mexico for winter.

2 Size _____ to a _____ millimetres wide.

3 Total distance travelled _____ kilometres.

4 They travel _____ to _____ kilometres a day.

5 Predators eat _____ of Monarchs in winter.

6 _____ Monarchs died in rain storms last winter.

3 Read the article again. Are the sentences true (T) or false (F)?

1 The bright colours of the Monarch butterfly has a special meaning for predators. ___

2 The maximum length of a Monarch butterfly's life is five weeks. ___

3 It is usual for all species of butterflies to have winter and summer habitats. ___

4 When they travel to Mexico, Monarchs all follow the same route. ___

5 The monarch butterfly only eats poisonous plants. ___

6 Monarch butterflies can survive in cold and wet weather conditions. ___

7 Monarch butterflies may be endangered in the future because their habitat is disappearing. ___

8 The Mexican government wants to protect the Monarch's winter habitat. ___

The Monarch Butterfly

The Monarch butterfly is one of the most beautiful insects on our planet. It lives in North and South America and in autumn, about 100 million monarchs travel to their winter habitat in Mexico. The Monarch has orange, black and white wings and they are about ninety to a hundred millimetres wide. The bright colours tell predators that the Monarch tastes horrible and is poisonous.

Each year, four to five generations of Monarchs are born. Most of them live only two to five weeks, but the last generation of the summer lives for six to seven months. These long-living butterflies make the long journey from North America to the centre of Mexico. They travel three thousand five hundred kilometres or more.

Scientists believe that Monarch butterflies are the only species of butterfly that travel between a summer habitat and a winter habitat. They usually travel about eighty kilometres a day. However, some butterflies fly nearly 130 kilometres in a day. Monarchs fly alone but on the same path. They only fly during the day, following the sun and at night they stop in forests with other Monarchs. During this period, one tree may have thousands of butterflies on it. There are about fourteen different forests where they usually stop on their way to Mexico.

Monarchs are plant eaters. They spend most of the spring and summer looking for and eating food. One of the plants it eats has poison in it. This poison doesn't hurt the Monarchs, but it makes them taste terrible. For this reason, most birds do not eat Monarchs. However, during winter, predators eat about fourteen percent of Monarchs. Recently, extreme weather conditions have been a problem for the butterflies. Heavy rain in Mexico killed about fifty percent of the Monarch population last winter. If the winters become wet and cold because of climate change, the Monarchs will freeze to death.

The Monarch is not endangered, but unfortunately, its habitat is in danger at the moment. Modern farming has changed their habitat and many flowers and trees have disappeared. The Mexican government have created a programme to protect the habitats of the Monarch butterfly. They will help to protect the forest that is their home during the winter. Without this, the Monarchs will not survive.

Listening

4 **2.12** **Listen to the conversation and complete the notes.**

Dolphins

1 _____ are fish.

2 Dolphins are _____ .

3 There are _____ species of dolphins.

4 The closest land relative to the dolphin is a _____ .

5 The biggest mammal on Earth is _____ .

6 A baby dolphin is called a _____ .

5 **2.12** **Listen again and guess the meaning of the words (1–8).**

1 **cruise**   **a** a journey on a ship
               b a journey on a train
               c a journey on a plane

2 **flippers**   **a** body parts like wings
               b body parts like arms
               c body parts like ears

3 **fin**   **a** eyes
               b tail
               c thin flat part that sticks out of a fish

4 **clue**   **a** the answer
               b extra time
               c a helpful piece of information

5 **go on**   **a** continue   **b** stop   **c** have a break

6 **tricky**   **a** easy   **b** funny   **c** difficult

Use of English

6 **Complete the emails with the correct words.**

| From: | Casper > Casper11@usa3.com |
| To: | Tom > Tom-Clancy@hotmail2.com |

Hi Casper,

Today I came ¹_____ an old book in the second hand book shop. It looked interesting and none ²_____ the other books were very good, so I bought it. It's great. I'm reading it so quickly that I'm going ³_____ finish it today or tomorrow. It's called *Under the Frog* and it's about some Hungarian basketball players. I don't know if there's a film of the book. ⁴_____ there is, I'll definitely get it from the DVD shop on Friday. ⁵_____ don't you come round and watch it with me? We can always get a different film if we can't find that one.

Tom

| From: | Tom > Tom-Clancy@hotmail2.com |
| To: | Casper > Casper11@usa3.com |

Hi Tom,

Thanks for the email but I don't think I ⁶_____ be able to come to your house this weekend. I've ⁷_____ flu all week. I'm getting better now but I still ⁸_____ weak. The doctor gave me some medicine and I'm still ⁹_____ that. I think I need to rest for a few more days. What ¹⁰_____ watching a film next week?

Casper

Exam Choice 4

Speaking

7 **2.13** Complete the dialogue with the correct words. Then listen and check.

A: Why ¹_____ we do something one evening?

B: ²_____?

A: I think we ³_____ go out for a pizza.

B: ⁴_____?

A: What ⁵_____ tomorrow night.

B: ⁶_____?

A: Because we haven't had pizza for ages. ⁷_____ invite a few friends.

B: ⁸_____?

A: Amy, Sam, Emily and Josh. We ⁹_____ meet in town.

B: ¹⁰_____?

A: Near the bus station.

B: Okay, great!

8 Write a dialogue arranging a day trip, a weekend trip or a holiday. Include short questions as in Exercise 7.

Writing

9 Complete the instructions for joining Animal Rescue International. Use the linkers in the box.

Then   Second   Finally   First

How to join
Animal Rescue International

1 _____ you need to be sure that you want to do this. Read the website carefully and read about other people's experiences.

2 _____ discuss it with your parents. You will need their help and support.

3 _____ choose the right project for you. Think about the things you enjoy doing most and find the project that suits you.

4 _____, fill in the application form on the website. We will get back to you as soon as we can.

10 Look at the pictures and put the instructions (a-e) in the correct order.

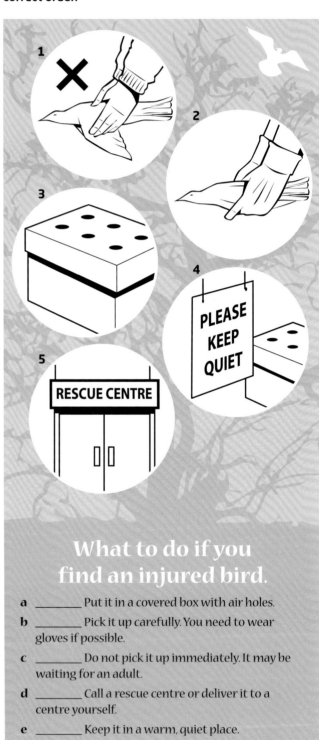

What to do if you find an injured bird.

a _____ Put it in a covered box with air holes.

b _____ Pick it up carefully. You need to wear gloves if possible.

c _____ Do not pick it up immediately. It may be waiting for an adult.

d _____ Call a rescue centre or deliver it to a centre yourself.

e _____ Keep it in a warm, quiet place.

11 Complete the instructions with the linkers in the box.

Second   Then   Third   First   Finally

TOPIC TALK - VOCABULARY

1 Use the clues to complete the puzzle about different forms of transport. What is the hidden word?

1 Kawasaki, Triumph, Moto Guzzi are examples of this.
2 Walking means you are on …
3 This machine flies without wings.
4 Boeing and Airbus make these.
5 A bike with a small engine.
6 A train below the surface.
7 This carries passengers on the road.
8 Ride on this in the Tour de France.
9 Something to travel on water.
10 A train on city streets.
11 A small boat on a fast river.
12 Riding usually means you are on …

1 m o t o r b i k e

2 Complete the sentences with the correct preposition.

1 I don't go to school ___on___ foot.
2 My mother goes to work _____ train.
3 It takes me _____ twenty minutes to get to the city centre.
4 We always go _____ holiday by car.
5 I've never been _____ an aeroplane.
6 My friend goes to school on _____ underground.

3 Complete the dialogue with the correct words.

A: How was school today?
B: Okay, but I arrived late.
A: Did you ¹___go___ to school ²_____ foot?
B: No, it was raining so I went ³_____ bus and it ⁴_____ me more than an hour.
A: An hour! You should go by bike. Charlie goes to school by bike every day and it only ⁵_____ him twenty minutes. It's convenient and it's good exercise, too.
B: I don't like exercise and I ⁶_____ cycling. I'd like ⁷_____ get a moped.
A: Well, they're quicker but they're expensive, and in my opinion they're dangerous.
B: Lots of my friends go to school ⁸_____ moped and they're never late for class.

4 Complete the sentences with the correct words from below.

~~convenient~~ crowds delays queues quick uncomfortable seats

1 I love my bike because it's so _convenient_: I can cycle anywhere I want and I never have problems parking.
2 I hate cheap airlines because of the _____. I'm very tall and I don't have enough space for my legs.
3 I always go to school on the underground because it's _____. The same journey takes me twice as long on the bus.
4 I can't stand trains because of the _____. The trains in this country are never on time.
5 I hate late night buses because of the _____. Sometimes there are over a 100 people waiting for one bus.
6 I don't like airport arrivals because of the _____. There are always hundreds of people waiting at the arrivals gate and you have to walk through the middle of them.

1 Read the article and find four names for people employed to look after passengers on an aeroplane.

1 _steward_ 3 _____
2 _____ 4 _____

The first
flight
attendant

In the 1920s and 30s the airlines were just beginning. It was unusual for people to travel by air because it was expensive, uncomfortable and dangerous. **1** ___f___ Young men, or 'stewards' helped the passengers onto the aeroplane and carried *the passengers'* luggage but they did not provide food and drinks. But then, in 1930, a woman called Ellen Church invented the 'stewardess'.

Ellen Church was born in 1904 on a farm in Iowa. She was an unconventional child. **2** _____ Ellen studied to be a nurse at the University of Minnesota and then got a job in a hospital. For the next few years she stayed at the hospital but also took flying lessons and got her pilot's license.

Ellen was twenty-five-years old when she first contacted Boeing Air Transport. **3** _____ Although women like Emelia Earheart were becoming famous, she realised it was impossible for a woman to have a career as a pilot. But she had another idea. Most people were frightened of flying because flying was still an unreliable way to travel. There were often delays, many crashes and the bad weather made many passengers sick. Ellen thought nurses could take care of passengers during flights and B.A.T. agreed.

The young woman from Iowa and seven other nurses became the first air stewardesses.

At first pilots were unhappy because they did not want stewardesses on aeroplanes, but passengers loved the stewardesses. In 1940 there were around 1000 of them working for different airlines. The original 'stewardess' had to be under twenty-five-years-old, single and slim. When a woman joined an airline, she had to promise not to get married or have children. It was a hard job and not well paid. **4** _____

In the 1970s, stewardesses were unhappy in their job and airlines had to make some changes. Since the 1970s, 'stewards' and 'stewardesses' have been called flight attendants or cabin crew. **5** _____

The first 'stewardess', Ellen Church, finally became a pilot when she worked as a captain in the Army. Unfortunately, she died in 1965 after a horse riding accident.

2 Match the sentences (a–f) with the gaps (1–5) in the text. There is one extra sentence.

a She didn't want to work on a farm or marry a farmer – she wanted a more adventurous life.

b They earn a good salary and work fewer hours than in the past.

c She loved flying but she understood that airlines were a man's world.

d Most airlines only provided one flight attendant for every fifty seats.

e They worked long hours and earned only $1 an hour.

f In those days, there were no flight attendants to look after the passengers.

Word Builder Opposites

3 Find the opposites of the adjectives below in the article on the left. Which opposite is formed differently from the others?

1 usual _unusual_
2 comfortable _____
3 conventional _____
4 possible _____
5 reliable _____
6 happy _____

4 Complete the sentences using the positive or negative form of the adjectives from Exercise 3.

1 I was a _conventional_ child. I wanted to grow up and be just like my father.
2 I hate travelling by air – seats are so small and _____.
3 I really want to be a pilot, but I think it may be _____ because I wear glasses.
4 Even today, it's _____ to see a female pilot on a commercial airline.
5 The trains in my country are extremely _____. They always leave and arrive exactly on time.
6 I'm a nervous flyer – I'm always _____ when the plane lands safely.

Writing

5 Read the text on the right. Which of these men was the first person to fly from France to England?

a Orville Wright
b Wilbur Wright
c Hubert Lathan
d Louis Bleriot

6 Find the following reference words in the text on the right. What or who do they refer to?

1 he (line 8)
2 they (line 13)
3 These brave men (line 16)
4 the trip (line 28)
5 him (line 39)

7 Replace the underlined words in the text on the right with the reference words below.

another   he   him   it   that   their   then
there   ~~they~~

In 1908, Lord Northcliffe, the owner of the Daily Mail newspaper, offered a prize of £500 for the first person
5 to fly across the English Channel. At first, nobody was interested in the race, so **he** offered £1000.

At the time, everybody thought that the Wright
10 brothers, Orville and Wilbur, could win the race. But ¹Orville and Wilbur Wright ___they___ thought ²the race _____ was too dangerous because the engines on the planes were unreliable. **They** often ran out of fuel and caused a lot of crashes.

15 By the middle of the following year, two French pilots were interested in the race. **These brave men** were pioneers in the world of flying.

An Anglo/French businessman called Hubert Latham was the first person to try and make a
20 flight across the Channel. ³Hubert Lathan _____ was brought up in France but went to Oxford University. After ⁴studying at Oxford, _____ he went to flying school in France. While he was ⁵at flying school in France _____ he became
25 ⁶the flying school's _____ principal flying teacher.

On 19th July 1909, early in the morning, he started the flight from France to England, but only thirteen kilometres into **the trip**, the engine stopped. Latham landed on the sea and a ship rescued
30 ⁷Latham _____ a few minutes later. He became the first person to land a plane on the sea. After the first flight he made ⁸a second _____ flight but crashed into the sea again.

On 25 July 1909 a French man called Louis Bleriot
35 left France in his plane. His flight was successful, and he arrived in Dover thirty-seven minutes later. Since ⁹25 July 1909 _____ he has been famous as the first person to fly across the English Channel. The French were proud of **him**, and England was
40 no longer an island!

26 GRAMMAR
The Passive

REMEMBER

Complete exercises A–C before you start this lesson.

Ⓐ Underline the correct form. How many sentences are in the Passive?

1 Airline meals *usually prepare/are usually prepared* on the ground and then reheated in the air.
2 Over 200,000 people *employ/are employed* in preparing food for airlines.
3 Singapore Airlines *spends/is spent* about $700million on food every year.
4 At Delta Airlines more than $8million *spends/is spent* on wine alone.
5 An aeroplane flying from Europe to Australia *carries/is carried* over 1000 kilograms of food.
6 Each year, over 500,000 boxes of chocolates *give/are given* to BA passengers.

Ⓑ Complete the sentences with the Passive form of the words in brackets.

1 My mum *is employed* at the local primary school. (employ)
2 I _____ by birds singing every morning. (wake up)
3 My parents _____ at the end of every month. (pay)
4 My name _____ the same way in English. (not spell)
5 Films _____ in their original version at my local cinema. (not show)
6 Our rubbish _____ every Friday morning. (collect)

Ⓒ Write Passive sentences. Use the underlined word as the subject of the question.

1 Do they build aeroplanes in your country?
   Are aeroplanes built in your country?
2 Do they make cars in your country?
   _____
3 Do they grow rice in your country?
   _____
4 Do they produce wine in your country?
   _____
5 Do they teach English at primary school in your country?
   _____
6 Do they pay teachers well in your country?
   _____

❶ * Complete the facts about Heathrow Airport with the correct form of the verbs in brackets.

1 London Heathrow Airport *was officially opened* (officially open) in 1946.
2 The airport _____ (locate) twenty-four kilometres west of central London.
3 Currently, 72,000 people _____ (employ) at the airport.
4 28,000 bags _____ (lose) on the opening day at the new Terminal 5.
5 Since Terminal 5 opened, nearly 5,000 of those 28,000 bags _____. (destroy)
6 A decision _____ (made) not to build a third runway at Heathrow.

Sentence Builder *by* phrases

❷ ** Write Passive sentences. Use the underlined word as the subject of the question. Use *by* + phrase to say who did it.

1 Did your grandparents build your house?
   Was your house built by your grandparents?
2 Did your mum make your lunch?
   _____
3 Has a dog ever bitten you?
   _____
4 Does the government employ your father?
   _____
5 Do foreigners pronounce your name correctly?
   _____
6 Has a policeman ever stopped you?
   _____
7 Did your dad bring you to school?
   _____
8 Did your brother buy you this mobile phone?
   _____

3 ** Use the cues to write questions in the Passive. Then match the questions (1-6) with the answers (a-f).

1 Where / build / Boeing aeroplanes?

_____ *Where are Boeing aeroplanes built?* _____ _b_

2 When / invent / the jet engine?

_____ ___

3 When / launch / the first satellite?

_____ ___

4 What / call / the first satellite?

_____ ___

5 How much / spend / on space exploration / since 1958?

_____ ___

6 Which vegetable / grow / in space?

_____ ___

a Sputnik
b Washington, USA
c Over \$800 billion
d The potato
e 1957
f 1930

4 *** Complete the text with the Active or Passive form of the verbs at the end of each line.

The first woman in space

On 16 June 1963 Vostock 6 [1] *was successfully launched* and   launch
Russian Cosmonaut, Valentina Tereshkova
[2] _____ the first woman in space. An   become
expert parachutist, Tereshkova [3] _____ by   inspire
the flight of Yuri Gagarin – the first man in space – and
[4] _____ for the cosmonaut program in   accept
1961. It is said that Tereshkova [5] _____   choose
for the historic flight because she [6] _____   be
the 'best communist', rather than the 'best cosmonaut'. After
the flight she [7] _____ a hero of the Soviet   name
Union and [8] _____ the Order of Lenin on   give
two occasions. Since she stopped work in 1990 she
[9] _____ to appear at many space-related   ask
events. She still [10] _____ to be a Russian   consider
hero.

For her 70th birthday she [11] _____ to   invite
Vladimir Putin's house and said that she would like to fly to
Mars, even if it is only a one-way trip.

Grammar Alive The news

5 *** Use the cues to write a news item. Use correct tenses and the Passive where necessary.

Last Tuesday a US communications satellite - hit by
an old Russian satellite. - Both satellites completely
destroyed - a large amount of space junk produced by
the crash. - The junk watched by the Americans since the
accident - so far, no other satellites damaged. - Since the
first Sputnik launched in 1957, NASA estimates that over
4000 satellites put into space. - Only about half of these
satellites currently used. - The others just left in orbit to
add to the space junk mountain.

Last Tuesday a US communications satellite was
hit by an old ... _____
_____
_____
_____
_____

1 Put the phrases (a–i) in the correct order from departure to arrival at your destination.

   a wait in departure lounge or go shopping in duty free shops ☐

   b go to boarding gate ☐

   c arrive at the arrivals gate of your destination ☐

   d fly to your destination ☐

   e go to check-in ☐ 1

   f go through passport control ☐

   g go through customs ☐ 9

   h go through security control ☐

   i go to baggage reclaim ☐

2 **2.14** Complete the directions with the words below. Listen to check your answers.

in   through   between   ~~how~~   on
turn   of   past

A: Could you tell me ¹_how_ to get to the nearest bank?

B: Certainly sir. Go ²_____ security control and ³_____ right. Go ⁴_____ the toilets and a bookshop. The bank is ⁵_____ your right, ⁶_____ the souvenir shop and the restaurant. It's ⁷_____ front ⁸_____ the duty free shops.

3 **2.15** Listen to the airport situation. Are the sentences true (T) or false (F)?

   1 The woman had the wrong ticket. ___

   2 The woman had her husband's passport. ___

   3 She asks for an aisle seat. ___

   4 She's got a suitcase and three bags. ___

   5 She pays excess baggage. ___

   6 She asks for directions to the information desk. ___

4 **2.15** Replace the <u>underlined</u> requests and responses with more formal language. Then listen to the dialogue again and check your answers.

Certainly ~~Could I~~ Could you Sorry, I can't.
Just a moment. Not at all madam.
Yes, here you are. Yes, I did.

A: ¹<u>Can I</u> _Could I_ have your passport and ticket please.

B: ²<u>Yes.</u> _____

A: I'm afraid you can't travel without your passport madam. Are you sure you haven't got it?

B: ³<u>Wait.</u> _____ Oh yes, here it is.

A: ⁴<u>Can you</u> _____ put your case here, please?

B: ⁵<u>No.</u> _____

A: Did you pack the suitcase yourself?

B: ⁶<u>Yes.</u> _____

A: Could you tell me how to get to a Post Office?

B: ⁷<u>Yes.</u> _____

A: Thanks a lot.

B: ⁸<u>That's okay.</u> _____

5 **2.16** Complete the directions with the correct words. Then, listen and check your answers.

Female: Okay, thanks. Oh, could you tell me how to get to a Post Office. I need to post my husband's passport to him.

Male: Certainly. There's one near ¹_to_ the information desk. Go to the end ²_____ check-in and turn right. It's next ³_____ the newsagents, in front ⁴_____ the information desk.

Female: Okay, to the end of check-in, ⁵_____ right and it's near to the newsagents ⁶_____ front of the information desk.

Check Your Progress 9

1 Journeys **Complete the text with the correct prepositions.**

How many adults do you know who travel ¹_____ work ²_____ bus or ³_____ train? All my friends' parents go to work ⁴_____ car, and usually there's just one person in each car. My mother works about five kilometres from our house – why doesn't she go ⁵_____ bike? When my father goes ⁶_____ a foreign country, of course he has to go ⁷_____ plane. But when he needs to go to the office, he could go ⁸_____ the underground but he says it's too far. I hope people my age will think more about the environment and leave their cars at home.

/8

2 Opposites **Complete the opposites of the adjectives below. Then complete the sentences.**

__experienced   __happy   __lucky   __possible
__reliable   __usual

1 Flying to Mars is an _____ dream.
2 My car is very _____. Sometimes it starts, sometimes it doesn't.
3 Many people think thirteen is _____. I don't.
4 Gus is a very _____ pilot. He only started flying a few months ago.
5 Sam, you look _____. Is something wrong?
6 She has an _____ name. I've never heard it before.

/6

3 The Passive **Write Passive sentences.**

1 They built my house in 1974.
   My house _____ _____ in 1974.
2 They have sold all the tickets.
   All the tickets _____.
3 They designed the airplane to carry 150 passengers.
   The airplane _____ to carry 150 passengers.
4 They make my phone in Japan.
   My phone _____ in Japan
5 They stole a laptop yesterday afternoon.
   A laptop _____ yesterday afternoon.
6 They cook hot food at school. Hot food _____ at school.
7 They have built a new road. A new road _____.

/7

4 The Passive - *by* phrases **Rewrite the sentences with the same meaning as the one above.**

1 BAA runs Heathrow Airport.
   Heathrow Airport _____
2 Millions of people have enjoyed the *Harry Potter* books.
   The *Harry Potter* books _____
3 Colin Firth played the part of King George VI.
   The part of King George VI _____
4 Heavy traffic causes a lot of air pollution.
   A lot of air pollution _____
5 Christopher Columbus didn't discover America.
   America _____
6 The new company designs websites.
   Websites _____

/6

5 Airport situations **Complete the dialogue with the correct words.**

A: ¹_____ your passport and ticket, please?
B: Yes, of course. Here ²_____.
A: ³_____ your case yourself?
B: Yes, ⁴_____.
A: Is that a window or ⁵_____?
B: Window, please.
A: ⁶_____ your case on here, please?
B: Sure.
A: Okay. ⁷_____ very much.
B: Thank you. ⁸_____.

/8

TOTAL SCORE /35

Module Diary 9

1 **Look at the objectives on page 69 in the Students' Book. Choose three and evaluate your learning.**

1 Now I can _____
   well / quite well / with problems.
2 Now I can _____
   well / quite well / with problems.
3 Now I can _____
   well / quite well / with problems.

2 **Look at your results. What language areas in this module do you need to study more?**

Sound Choice 5

Sound Check

Say the words and expressions below.

a It's made in China (Exercise 1)
b strong wasps (Exercise 2)
c crowd / boy / boat (Exercise 3)
d aisle / asthma / bomb (Exercise 4)
e Why don't you go? I think I should stay. (Exercise 5)
f cautious / funeral / convenient (Exercise 6)

(2.17) **Listen and check your answers. Which sounds and expressions did you have problems with? Choose three exercises to do below.**

1 (2.18) Grammar - contractions **Write the sentences with contractions. Then listen, check and repeat.**

1 It is made in China.
→ *It's made in China.*

2 I was not informed.
→ _____

3 They are used a lot.
→ _____

4 He has not been told.
→ _____

5 It has been damaged.
→ _____

6 They were not stolen.
→ _____

2 (2.19) Consonants - clusters with 's' **Practise saying the words. Then listen and repeat.**

1 strong wasps
2 snakes spray
3 stress tests
4 screen speed
5 sports score
6 smoke slow

3 (2.20) Vowels - diphthongs **Listen and repeat the words. Underline the word with a different vowel sound in each group.**

1 crowd / down / <u>know</u> / mouth / now
2 boy / coin / noise / out / toy
3 boat / join / load / rope / show

4 (2.21) Spelling - silent letters **Listen and repeat the words. Underline the silent letter(s) in each word.**

1 ai<u>s</u>le
2 asthma
3 bomb
4 flight
5 know
6 pneumonia
7 whale
8 write
9 yolk

5 (2.22) Expressions **Listen to the chants and underline the two stressed words/syllables on each line. Then practise repeating the chants.**

A
<u>Why</u> don't you <u>go</u>?
I think I should stay.
What about homework?
Let's leave it today.

B
I don't think we should stop,
I don't think we should stay.
Why don't we come back later?
We can come another day.

6 (2.23) Difficult words - word stress **Put the words into the correct column. Then listen, check and repeat.**

~~cautious~~   satellite   environment   funeral
parachute   patient   convenient   poisonous
ecologist   species   vicious   emergency

A ■■	B ■■■	C ■■■
cautious		

TOPIC TALK - VOCABULARY

1 Label the picture with the correct word or phrase.

b c_____

c f_____

f s_____

a b *each*_____

d s_____

e s_____

g s_____

2 Complete the lists with the words below.

apartment   bird-watching   castle   church   ~~hot spring~~
kayaking   lagoon   sailing   sight-seeing   snorkelling
stream   sunbathing

Describing water	*hot spring* _____ _____
Types of building	_____ _____ _____
Activities on water	_____ _____ _____
	_____ _____ _____
Activities on land	_____ _____ _____

3 Choose the correct word to complete the sentences.

1 We don't usually *go*/*go to* abroad for our holidays.
2 I've never been *on*/*to* holiday with the school.
3 My dream is to go to Bali because it's got a tropical *climate*/*weather*.
4 I'd like to stay *to*/*at* a campsite but I don't have a tent.
5 The last time I went *in*/*to* the coast was in August.
6 We usually stay *with*/*in* family when we go to my father's home town.

4 Complete the dialogue with the correct words below.

~~go on holiday~~   go to the coast
it's got beautiful beaches   My dream is to go to Florida
stay in an apartment   stayed at a campsite
stayed with my family   went sightseeing
went snorkelling   went to the country

A: Where do you usually ¹*go on holiday* Marta?

B: Every year we ²_____ and ³_____ but last year, for the first time, we went camping.

A: Oh really, where to?

B: We went to Corsica and ⁴_____.

A: What was that like?

B: Wonderful. The campsite was on the beach so we went swimming and sunbathing every day. I even ⁵_____ and saw some jellyfish.

A: Wow! Is Corsica nice?

B: Yes, ⁶_____ and some really high mountains with forests and mountain streams. My mum and dad left us on the beach a lot and ⁷_____. Dad loves visiting old churches and castles. What about you? What did you do?

A: Oh we ⁸_____ again and ⁹_____. It's the same every year. It's so boring. ¹⁰_____ but my parents say it's too expensive.

28 GRAMMAR
Unreal Conditional

REMEMBER

Complete exercises A–B before you start this lesson.

A Complete the sentences with the Future Conditional form of the words in brackets.

1 If you __like__ motorbikes, you_'ll love_ the new Triumph Daytona. (like / love)
2 Mum _____ you to the station, if you _____ ready to go now. (drive / be)
3 If we _____ the house now, we _____ the flight. (not leave / miss)
4 If you _____ your driving test, I _____ you a car. (pass / buy)
5 It _____ me about twenty minutes if I _____ by bus. (take / go)
6 If it _____ tomorrow, we _____ on the underground. (rain / go)

B Continue the story. Make sentences with *if*.

I'm late! I think I'm going to miss the school bus …

1 ➝ be late for school.
   If I miss the bus, I'll be late for school.
2 ➝ not go to English class.
   If I'm late for school, …
3 ➝ not practise speaking.
   _____
4 ➝ not get better.
   _____
5 ➝ fail my exam.
   _____

Complete exercises C–D before you start lesson 30.

C Complete the phrases with *a* or *an*.

1 __a__ kayak 2 _____ aeroplane
3 _____ delay 4 _____ hour 5 _____ exciting journey 6 _____ helicopter 7 _____ university 8 _____ uncomfortable seat

D Complete the sentences with *a, an, the* or (-).

1 __The__ bus station is in _____ city centre next to _____ train station.
2 My father is _____ engineer.
3 We haven't got _____ university in our city.
4 I speak _____ Spanish and _____ English.
5 I love _____ cars and _____ motorbikes
6 I go to _____ school on _____ foot but sometimes I use _____ underground.

① * Choose the correct words to complete the sentences.

1 If I (went)/would go to live on a desert island, I'd miss my laptop.
2 If I would appear/appeared on a reality show, I wouldn't tell my friends
3 I'd join a band if I had/would have a better singing voice.
4 If I would win/won the lottery, I'd share all the money with my family and friends.
5 If I could drive, I asked/'d ask my father to buy me a car.
6 I wouldn't study English if I didn't/wouldn't need it for my future.

② * Match the sentences in Exercise 1 to the meanings.

1 a present situation which is not true: __3__
   _____ _____ _____
2 an imaginary situation about the future: _____
   _____ _____

③ * Complete the questions with the correct form of the verbs in brackets. Then do the questionnaire.

1 If you __found__ a wallet in the street with some money in it, would you (find)
   a keep the wallet? b take it to a police station? c spend the cash and then take it to a police station?
2 If a friend _____ a bag at your house, would you (leave)
   a look through it? b call the friend immediately? c give it back the next time you saw the friend?
3 If a shop assistant _____ you too much change, would you (give)
   a keep the money? b tell him or her and give it back?
4 If you _____ a spider in the bath, would you (see)
   a kill it? b scream? c pick it up and put it outside?
5 If you _____ anywhere you wanted, would you live (can live)
   a in a city? b in the country? c in the mountains? d on the coast?

4 ** Write sentences saying what you would really do in the situations in the questionnaire in Exercise 3.

1 *If I found a wallet in the street with some money in it I'd …* _____

2 _____

3 _____

4 _____

5 _____

5 *** Rewrite the sentences with the same meaning as the one above.

1 My parents don't like foreign food so we don't go on holiday abroad.

If my parents liked foreign food, we'd go on holiday abroad.

2 I haven't got enough money so I can't buy a new mobile phone.

If _____, I _____

3 I can't go out because I've got so much homework.

I _____ if _____

4 I don't speak perfect English so I need to go to classes.

If _____, I _____

5 I don't download more films because I don't have a fast computer.

I _____ if _____

6 I feel sleepy because I always go to bed late.

I _____ if _____

7 I feel tired because I do a lot of sport.

If _____, I _____

8 I can't go to the concert because I have to help my parents.

If _____, I _____

Grammar Alive Dreaming

6 ** Jenny is a fifteen-year-old school girl who is dreaming of her perfect holiday. Complete the conditional sentences about her dreams.

Reality

she goes on holiday with her family

she goes to Wales

she stays at a campsite

the weather is awful

she can go sightseeing and visit old castles and churches

she always wants to go home

Dream

If Jenny was older and richer…,

she _would go on holiday with_ her boyfriend.

she _____ tropical island.

she _____ luxury hotel.

she _____ swimming with dolphins and snorkelling over coral reefs.

she _____

SKILLS
Listening

1 **2.24** Listen to the radio programme about Hawaii and look at the photos. Number them in the order you hear them mentioned.

a

b

c

2 **2.24** Listen to the programme again. Complete the notes below.

1 Hawaii became an American state in: _____
2 Summer temperature: _____ °C
3 Winter temperature: _____ °C
4 Number of main islands: _____
5 Population of Oahu: _____
6 The last big earthquake on the big island was in: _____

Word Builder Multi-part verbs (4)

3 Rewrite the underlined words with the correct form of the multi-part verbs below.

go out   go down   go up   go back   ~~go on~~

1 So what's <u>happening</u> in Hawaii, Jamie? *going on*
2 In summer, the temperature <u>increases</u> to 29.5°. _____
3 In winter it <u>decreases</u> to 25°. _____
4 Honolulu is a big modern city where people often <u>leave their homes and go somewhere to enjoy themselves</u>. _____
5 A lot of people were homeless for a while, but they've <u>returned</u> to their homes now. _____

Sentence Builder *-ing* forms

4 Complete sentences with the *-ing* form of the verbs below.

chill out   shop   whale-watch   climb   learn

1 When I'm on holiday I enjoy *shopping* to buy presents for my family.
2 I've never seen a whale – I really want to go _____ one day.
3 When I'm on holiday, I like new experiences like _____ to surf.
4 I'm not interested in sport when I'm on holiday. _____ on a beach is my favourite activity!
5 _____ a mountain is very hard work, but you get a fantastic view from the top!

5 Read the website about Hawaii. Which is the best island for activities 1-5 in Exercise 4? Put *O* for Oahu, *M* for Maui and *BI* for Big Island.

WELCOME TO HAWAII

Hawaii is a popular holiday destination. But which island should you choose for your holiday in paradise?

OAHU

All the international flights go from the capital, Honolulu, on Oahu Island. Oahu is the most populated island and home of the famous Waikiki beach. International surfing competitions take place here. Oahu is also the place for shops, restaurants and the best nightlife.

MAUI

Maui is the most romantic island and ideal for chilling out. There are white sandy beaches with turquoise water, and in summer the waves are small and perfect for inexperienced surfers. In winter, you can see whales in the warm water. Maui is ideal for nature lovers and visitors fall in love with the island's natural beauty.

BIG ISLAND

Big island is cheaper and for the more adventurous visitors. You can go to the top of the highest mountain 4000 metres above sea level and enjoy an amazing view.

GRAMMAR
the in geographical names

LESSON 30

Complete exercises C–D on page 84 before you start this lesson.

❶ Complete the geographical names with *the* or (-). Then match (1-6) with (a-f).

1 _the_ Amazon _f_   a _____ Europe
2 _____ Corsica ___   b _____ Indian Ocean
3 _____ Czech   c _____ London
   Republic ___   d _____ Mediterranean
4 _____ Maldives ___   e _____ New Zealand
5 _____ Thames ___   f _____ South America
6 _____ Waikato ___

❷ Complete the following facts with *the* or (-). Which 'fact' is false?

1 _The_ Nile is the longest river in _____-____ Africa.

2 _____ Mont Blanc is the highest mountain in _____ Alps.

3 _____ Hawaii is the smallest state in _____ USA.

4 _____ Sicily is the biggest island in _____ Mediterranean.

5 _____ Swansea (Wales) is the wettest city in _____ United Kingdom.

6 _____ Greenland is the largest island in _____ world.

❸ Complete the questions with *the* or (-).

1 Which sea is between ____-____ Poland and _____-____ Sweden?

2 Which country is between _____ Czech Republic and _____ Slovenia? _____

3 Which river flows from _____ Germany into _____ Black Sea? _____

4 Which mountain range lies between _____ Chile and _____ Argentina? _____

5 Which American state is between _____ Canada and _____ Russia? _____

6 Which river flows from _____ Himalayas into _____ Indian Ocean? _____

❹ Complete the geographical features with *the* or (-). Then match them to the correct sentences in Exercise 3.

a _____-_____ Alaska _5_
b _____ Andes ___
c _____ Austria ___
d _____ Baltic Sea ___
e _____ Danube ___
f _____ Ganges ___

❺ Read the text about the UK. Find where *the* is used incorrectly. There are twelve mistakes.

The United Kingdom

~~The~~ Great Britain is the largest island in the Europe. It includes the England, the Wales and the Scotland. The United Kingdom is slightly different from the Great Britain because it includes the Northern Ireland. So, the full official name of the country is the United Kingdom of Great Britain and Northern Ireland. The UK capital is the London where the River Thames flows into the North Sea. The Grampians in the Scotland are the highest mountains with the Ben Nevis at 1,344 metres, the highest peak. There are also many large lakes or 'lochs' in the Scotland including the most famous one, the Loch Ness. The Loch Ness Monster, sometimes known as 'Nessie', does not exist.

Workshop 5

Writing

1 **Read the postcard. Choose the correct words to complete the text.**

¹Dear/Hi Sophie
²Having a great time in/We are enjoying the Canary Islands. Now in Fuerteventura for a few days. Very windy – ³I am/I'm enjoying the windsurfing. Yesterday we were in Lanzarote. Saw the 'Fire Mountains' and hot springs and we even went on a CAMEL – very uncomfortable!! Lanzarote looks like the moon! Went horseriding on the beach this morning – AMAZING!! Tomorrow ⁴we're/we are going on a boat trip – hope we see some dolphins. Back on Sunday. ⁵See you/Look forward to seeing you next week.
⁶With best wishes/Take care, Anna
xxxx

Ms S. Soames
102 High Street
Witham
OB1 2QP

2 **Match the punctuation (1-5) with the meanings (a-e).**

1 CAPITAL LETTERS _b_
2 dashes (-) ___
3 Exclamation marks (!!!) ___
4 Contractions ___
5 xxxxx ___

a to comment on something mentioned
b to emphasise something
c to emphasise something
d kisses
e to show informal speech

3 **What words does Anna leave out? Complete the sentences.**

1 _I am_ having a great time in the Canary Islands.
2 _____ now in Fuerteventura.
3 _____ very windy.
4 _____ saw the Fire Mountains.
5 _____ very uncomfortable!
6 _____ went horseriding on the beach.
7 _____ hope we see some dolphins.
8 _____ back on Sunday.

4 **Complete the postcard with the correct punctuation.**

Hi Ollie, having a great time in Majorca now in the north the beaches are lovely very hot I'm enjoying swimming in the sea yesterday we visited some caves amazing tomorrow we're going diving hope we don't see any sharks back on Saturday see you next week take care Ruby xxxxx

Speaking

1 **2.25** **Listen to a dialogue about Phuket in a travel agent's and complete the notes.**

Rainy season: May to October
Best time to visit: ¹_November_ to April
Visa necessary?: ²_____
Price of a night in beach resort: ³£ _____ a night
Price of diving: ⁴£ _____ a day
Things to do: diving, ⁵_____, boat trip to other islands
Nature: ⁶_____, waterfalls, rainforest

2 **2.25** **Correct the mistakes in bold in the questions from the dialogue. Listen again and check your answers.**

1 Could you give me some information about Phuket, **right**? _please_
2 That's a good time to go, **no**? _____
3 I don't need a visa for two weeks, **don't I**? _____
4 Could you tell me about places to stay there, **yeah**? _____
5 Breakfast is included in the price, **don't you**? _____
6 Which resort **have you** recommend? _____
7 **Don't** you know anything about diving in Phuket? _____
8 There are lots of other things to do, **isn't it**? _____
9 **Have** you know anything about the nightlife?

Check Your Progress 10

1 Holidays **Complete the text with the correct words.**

When I was a child, I went ¹_____ holiday ²_____ my family every summer. We stayed ³_____ my grandparents in Cornwall. Cornwall's got some beautiful beaches and we often ⁴_____ swimming and surfing ⁵_____ the north coast. However, it rained a lot. I remember that my dream was to ⁶_____ to a place with a tropical ⁷_____ with coral ⁸_____, but Mum and Dad said they preferred England.

/8

2 Unreal Conditional **Complete the sentences with the correct form of the verbs in brackets.**

1 If I _____ enough money, I _____ buy a new laptop. (have / buy)
2 If I _____ an animal, I _____ a big black bear. (be / be)
3 Maria _____ better in class if she _____ so much. (do / not talk)
4 If Dave _____ the answer, I'm sure he _____ us. (know / tell)
5 My mum _____ if she _____. (not work / not have to)
6 If you _____ the President, what _____ you _____? (be / do)
7 I _____ you if I _____.(help / can)

/7

3 -ing forms **Complete the questions with the correct form of the words in brackets.**

1 What do you like about _____? (hike)
2 Do you think _____ is dangerous? (canoe)
3 Do you enjoy _____? (dance)
4 John can't stand _____? (swim)
5 What are you _____ at the moment? (study)
6 My brother loves _____ on holiday. (dive)
7 You can go _____ in the sea. (surf)

/7

4 Multi-part verbs (4) **Rewrite the underlined words with the correct form of the multi-part verb go.**

1 I don't usually socialise with my friends during the week.
2 What's happening? Why is there so much noise?
3 My neighbour never returns to the same place for a holiday.
4 The party continued until four in the morning.
5 House prices have never fallen.
6 Sea levels are rising because of global warming.

/6

5 the in geographical names **Complete the geographic names with the or (-).**

1 _____ Africa.
2 _____ Maldives.
3 _____ Amazon.
4 _____ Asia.
5 _____ Himalayas.
6 _____ Black Sea.
7 _____ Nile.

/7

TOTAL SCORE /35

Module Diary 10

1 **Look at the objectives on page 77 in the Students' Book. Choose three and evaluate your learning.**

1 Now I can _____
well / quite well / with problems.
2 Now I can _____
well / quite well / with problems.
3 Now I can _____
well / quite well / with problems.

2 **Look at your results. What language areas in this module do you need to study more?**

Exam Choice 5

Reading

❶ Read the text and answer the questions.

1 Where is the best place to build a shelter?
2 What kind of water is dangerous to drink?
3 Where is the best place to find food?

How to survive on a desert island

Nobody imagines that, one day, they might be **stranded** on a desert island – but it could happen. So it's a good idea to learn a few key skills that would help you to survive if it happened to you.

1 _____ The first thing you need to do is make a shelter on the beach, near the sea, so that you have a good view of any ships that pass your island. Your most important **task** is finding a way to get off the island, so you can't miss any **opportunities** of seeing somebody who could rescue you.

2 _____ It's a good idea to build your shelter near some trees. It will provide **shade** from the hot sun. If you get sunburned you won't be able to carry out the tasks you need to do to stay alive. If there are coconut trees, you could also use the oil from the coconut to protect your skin.

3 _____ Obviously you need to stay out of the way of any **harmful** animals or insects. Make a bed that is off the ground – you don't want to share your bed with snakes or other creepy crawlies.

4 _____ One of the most important things is to drink as much as you can. If you are out in the hot sun all day you will need about ten litres per day of fresh water. If you can't find a stream on the island, rain water will be your best chance of surviving. You need to make containers to catch and **store** rain water. Large plants with giant leaves are a good way to collect water. But never drink sea water – it will make you even more thirsty.

5 _____ The best **source** of food is probably the sea. You will need something to help you catch fish – for example, you could make a **spear** with a long branch from a tree. This will help you to catch the fish and bring it back to shore. If you have matches, or some other way of making a fire, it is safer to cook the fish than to eat it **raw.** However, fish can be eaten raw – think of sushi!

6 _____ Finally, you need to do anything possible to be seen and rescued. If you don't have what you need to make a fire, you can write 'HELP' on the beach using rocks to spell out the word.

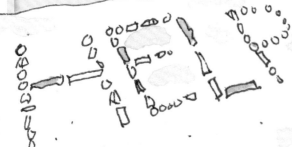

2 Match the headings (a-g) with the paragraphs (1-6). There is one extra heading.

a Make sure somebody sees you
b Get a roof over your head
c Build a boat
d Avoid dangerous wildlife
e Go fishing
f Use natural suntan lotion
g Drink plenty

3 Work out the meanings of the words in bold in the text.

1 stranded _____
2 task _____
3 opportunities _____
4 shade _____
5 harmful _____
6 store (vb) _____
7 source _____
8 spear _____
9 raw _____

Listening

4 2.26 Listen to the beginning of a news programme and choose the best headline.

a Surfers look for bigger waves.
b Boscombe to be surf capital of Europe.
c Artificial surf reef to make bigger waves.

5 2.27 Listen to the rest of the programme. Complete the sentences below.

1 The number of visitors has gone up by _____ percent.
2 Cost of the surf reef £ _____
3 Date it was opened November _____
4 Other surf reefs Australia, _____ and California
5 Distance from the beach _____ metres
6 Waves are up to _____ metres high.
7 Before the reef, number of good surfing days _____
8 After the reef, number of good surfing days _____
9 Number of surf visits to Boscombe this year _____

Speaking

6 2.28 Listen and complete the notes about Dublin.

1 Safe to cycle in Ireland? _____
2 Weather in July: _____
3 Towns to visit Dublin, _____ Galway
4 Irish people _____, talkative.
5 Cost of return flight: € _____
6 Flight dates To Dublin _____, return _____

7 2.28 Choose the correct words to complete the questions. Listen again and check your answers.

1 Hello could you give me some information about Ireland, _____?
   a isn't it   b please
2 It's safe to cycle around Ireland, _____?
   a isn't it   b no
3 The weather's okay in July, _____?
   a aren't they   b right
4 Could you tell me about places to visit in Ireland, _____?
   a please   b right
5 There are lots of things to see, _____?
   a isn't it   b aren't there
6 Irish people are friendly, _____?
   a don't they   b right
7 Could you give me some information about flights, _____?
   a couldn't you   b please
8 The nineteenth is a Sunday, _____?
   a isn't it   b don't you

Exam Choice 5

Use of English

8 Complete the second sentence so that it has the same meaning as the one above. Use between two to five words including the word in capitals.

1 We ask passengers to check-in two hours before their flight.
ASKED
Passengers _____ to check-in two hours before their flight.

2 The only thing stopping me from going to the Maldives is that I haven't got any money.
LOT
If _____ of money, I'd go to the Maldives.

3 What's happening? The queue for check-in hasn't moved for ages.
ON
What's _____? The queue for check-in hasn't moved for ages.

4 Do you really believe there is life on other planets?
YOU
_____ there is life on other planets, do you?

5 The people at security control stopped my dad last summer.
STOPPED
My dad _____ at control last summer.

6 I hope you haven't forgotten our passports.
YOU
You haven't forgotten our passports, _____?

7 A tsunami has destroyed the village.
BEEN
The village _____ a tsunami.

8 You only have to pay extra because your bags are so heavy.
WEREN'T
If your bags _____ have to pay extra.

9 If the sea level rises by just ten centimetres, lots of people will lose their homes.
GOES
If the sea level _____ by just ten centimetres, lots of people will lose their homes.

10 Someone has taken our passports.
BEEN
Our passports _____.

Writing

9 Read the text about Phi Phi island. What are the two events that made it famous?

Phi Phi island is Thailand's island superstar. **¹Phi Phi island** has long white sandy beaches, turquoise sea, mountains, caves and a coral reef. You can climb, dive, snorkel, explore the island by kayak or canoe, swim in the warm water or chill out on one of the wonderful beaches. Fishermen first populated the island in the 1940s.

Phi Phi island first became famous when Leonardo Di Caprio, filmed The Beach ²**on Phi Phi island** in 1999. Newspapers reported that the film company damaged the island, but ³**the film company** have always said that this wasn't true.

Tragically, the Asian tsunami badly damaged Phi Phi in 2004. About seventy per cent of the buildings on the island were destroyed. After ⁴**the tsunami**, the Thai government closed the island. Local people and foreign volunteers created 'Help International Phi Phi'. ⁵**'Help International Phi Phi'** cleaned the beaches and helped to rebuild houses. After the tsunami, people were frightened that there would be another ⁶**tsunami**. So a tsunami alarm system was placed on Phi Phi by the Thai government.

10 Replace the words in italics with the reference words below.

it   one   that   there   they   they

11 Choose the correct words to complete the sentences.

1 Last year we went on holiday to Thailand for three weeks. *It/there* was wonderful.

2 We stayed in small huts on the beach. *There/They* didn't have electricity.

3 We started our holiday on a small island and then after a week we moved to a bigger *them/one*.

4 The first time I went to the beach I got sunburnt so after *that/then* I stayed out of the sun.

5 I wanted to go diving, but unfortunately *it/he* was too expensive.

12 Write similar sentences about a holiday you've been on.

TOPIC TALK – VOCABULARY

1 Match the adjectives (1-7) with the opposite meaning (a-g).

1 talkative _c_   a moody
2 slim ___   b lazy
3 good-looking ___   c quiet
4 easy-going ___   d shy
5 hard-working ___   e untidy
6 tidy ___   f ugly
7 outgoing ___   g overweight

2 Complete the meanings with the words below.

> confident   impatient   ~~sensible~~   sensitive
> sociable

1 _sensible_ able to make good decisions
2 _____ easily offended or upset
3 _____ friendly and enjoys being with people
4 _____ sure that he or she can do something well
5 _____ angry because he or she has to wait

3 <u>Underline</u> the adjective with a negative meaning.

1 slim   <u>skinny</u>   tall   well-built
2 sensible   honest   impatient   confident
3 moody   helpful   enthusiastic   friendly
4 handsome   pretty   ugly   attractive

4 Choose the correct words to complete the text.

Rose is a good friend of ¹(mine)/me. ²We've known/We know each other for four years. We met when I was on holiday in Scotland. She's very pretty – I think so anyway. She's ³too/quite short and slim and ⁴she is/she's got long hair – her hair's beautiful, and it isn't ⁵dyed/wavy. It's completely natural! She's really friendly and outgoing. She loves parties and she'll talk to anybody! In fact, she's very talkative – we have really long phone conversations. Sometimes she's ⁶a bit/a lot moody, and then she's quiet and doesn't want to chat. But it doesn't happen very often.

5 Complete the text with the correct words.

Freddie is a very good friend ¹ _of_ mine. I ²_____ known him all my life – our mothers were friends before we were born. Some people think we're brothers. I don't know why – I ³_____ very good-looking and he's really ugly! Ha ha, not really. In fact, girls think he's attractive. He's tall, quite skinny and he's ⁴_____ short dark ⁵_____. People think he's really confident, but in fact he's quite shy. I love spending time with him because he's really funny. We laugh at the same things. Sometimes he's ⁶_____ bit too sensitive and I have to be careful what I say, but most of the time we have a great time together.

31

SKILLS
Reading

1 Read the text. Where would you find an article like this?

a in a brochure
b in a film magazine
c on a website

2 What is the purpose of the article?

a To give an opinion about the film.
b To compare the film characters with the real people.
c To tell the story of Facebook.

FILM NEWS
The Social Network: A Story of Friendship

The Social Network tells the story of Facebook, the social networking site. But it is also a film about friendship, and loss of friendship, among a group of University students.

The characters in the film are based on real people, but how similar are the film characters and the real people?

Jesse Eisenberg, the actor who plays Facebook founder Mark Zuckerberg, is better looking than Zuckerberg, but in most ways, they look very similar: they are both pale skinned and have curly hair; they are both one metre seventy-five centimetres tall and Eisenberg is just six months older than Zuckerberg.

In the film Zuckerberg always wears casual clothes. He even goes to one important meeting in his pyjamas. The real Zuckerberg confirms that this actually happened, and he recognises his own clothes in the film. 'It's interesting that every single shirt and fleece* is actually a shirt or fleece that I own,' he commented.

However, he says that the similarity ends there. In the film Zuckerberg is a loner with just one close friend. The film also suggests that he creates Facebook because he's angry with an ex-girlfriend.

In fact, people who know the real Zuckerberg say that he is a confident young man, not very talkative, but very intelligent and extremely hard-working. He gets on well with his family and friends, and has had the same girlfriend since he was at Harvard. Zuckerberg comments that the film makes the story of Facebook more exciting than it really was. 'I'm just a little kid,' he told an interviewer, 'I get bored easily and computers excite me.'

Zuckerberg's best friend, Eduardo Saverin is played by Andrew Garfield. The actor looks very similar to the real person – tall, slim, good-looking with dark eyes and dark brown hair. In the film, he is kind, honest, helpful and sensitive, and friends say that this is true of the real Saverin. He invests in Facebook and becomes Zuckerberg's business partner, but after an argument, Zuckerberg gets rid of him.

The other main characters in the film are the Winklevoss twins who accuse Zuckerberg of stealing the idea for Facebook from them. The twins are one metre ninety-six centimetres, blond, handsome, sporty and extremely confident. It was impossible to find similar twin actors, so Armie Hammer, who's also one metre ninety-six centimetres, handsome and blond, plays both parts. When he was filming *The Social Network*, he became friends with the Winklevoss brothers on Facebook!

Click here for an interview with David Fincher, Director of *The Social Network*.

* **fleece** a jacket made of soft, warm material

3 Answer the questions.

1 In what ways do Jesse Eisenberg and Mark Zuckerberg look different, and in what ways do they look similar?
2 Who does Zuckerberg get angry with in the film?
3 According to Zuckerberg, what is more exciting – the film story of Facebook or the real story?
4 Who gets bored easily?
5 Who does Zuckerberg get rid of from Facebook?

Word Builder *get*

4 Complete the text with the words below.

getting on   got angry   ~~getting bored~~   get your clothes
get on   get rid of   getting really good marks   get angry

Last summer I was ¹*getting bored* so I started French classes. There are twelve of us in the class and I ²_____ with everyone, except one girl. At first we were ³_____ okay, but then I started ⁴_____ and she didn't like that. She ⁵_____ with me and said horrible things. One day she asked me, 'where do you ⁶_____?' I told her the name of my favourite shop, and she said, 'Thanks – I'll make sure I don't go there.' I'm quite confident, so I didn't ⁷_____. She's the one with problems – I hope she ⁸_____ her negative attitude soon.

Sentence Builder *as* for comparisons

5 Use the cues to write sentences using *as/not as*.

1 Mark Zuckerberg / good-looking / Jesse Eisenberg
   Mark Zuckerberg isn't as good-looking as
   Jesse Eisenberg.
2 Mark Zuckerberg / old / Jesse Eisenberg
   _____
3 Mark Zuckerberg / unfriendly / his character in the film
   _____
4 The real story of Facebook / exciting / the film story of Facebook
   _____
5 The character played by Andrew Garfield / nice / the real Eduardo Saverin
   _____
6 Armie Hammer / tall / the Winklevoss twins
   _____

Writing

6 Complete the text below with the words in brackets. Use *as/not as*.

Colin Firth was born in 1960. He has short dark wavy hair and he is quite tall. He is an actor and he won his first Oscar in 2011 for *The Kings Speech*. He lives in London with his Italian wife.

Ewan McGregor was born in 1971 so he ¹*isn't as old as* (old) Colin Firth. He has got short, brown hair but I don't think he ²_____ (tall) Firth. He is also an actor and he is probably ³_____ (good) Colin Firth but he hasn't won an Oscar yet. He lives in California and he is a very private person – I don't think he is ⁴_____ (open) Firth.

7 Write about two of the celebrities below or a celebrity from your country.

Hugh Grant   Daniel Radcliffe   Tom Cruise   Matt Damon
Keira Knightley   Natalie Portman   Nicole Kidman

_____
_____
_____
_____
_____
_____
_____

GRAMMAR
Intentions and arrangements

Complete exercises A–C before you start this lesson.

A Complete the text with the Present Continuous form of the words in brackets.

I'm so excited about our skiing holiday. We
¹ *'re going* (go) to La Plagne in the French Alps. I
² _____ (go) with three friends and we
³ _____ (leave) next Saturday. We ⁴ _____
(take) the Snow Train from London and we
⁵ _____ (stay) at a friend's apartment. I'm the
only one who's never skied before but I ⁶ _____
(have) lessons every morning. I ⁷ _____ (not
come back) until I can ski!

B Use the cues to write questions and short answers. Use the Present Continuous.

1 you / have lunch / after this lesson? Yes / No
   Are you having lunch after this lesson?
   Yes, I am. No, I'm not.

2 you / do anything / after school? Yes / No
   _____

3 your parents / go out / this evening? Yes / No
   _____

4 you / take any exams / next week? Yes / No
   _____

5 your best friend / come to your house / on Friday? Yes / No
   _____

6 you / meet your friends in town / on Saturday? Yes / No
   _____

C Rewrite the questions or sentences with *be going to*.

1 I plan to buy a new laptop next year.
   I'm going to buy a new laptop next year.

2 Tom has decided not to join the gym.
   _____

3 What are your plans after you leave school?
   _____

4 Do you intend to go to university?
   _____

5 Emily has decided to study French.
   _____

6 I've decided not to eat any more junk food.
   _____

❶ * Complete the New Year resolutions with *be going to* and the verbs below.

~~change~~   not eat   get   join   spend   not watch

New Year's Resolutions

It's 31 December ...
1 Maria *is going to change* her hairstyle.
2 Brad _____ less time online.
3 Anna _____ a new mobile phone.
4 Jamie _____ so much fast food.
5 Sarah _____ so much television.

2 ** Look at Jo's diary. Complete the dialogue with the Present Continuous and the correct form of the verbs from the diary.

Saturday

10.00	shopping with mum
1.00	have lunch with Andy
2.30	swimming with Andy
5.00	meet Sarah and Lisa in town
7.00	eat dinner at Grandpa's
9.00	go to party at Andy's

Jamie: [1] *Are you doing* anything on Saturday? We could meet up for a coffee or something.

Jo: Actually, I'm quite busy this Saturday.

Jamie: What about the morning?

Jo: Sorry, I can't. I [2]_____ with Mum.

Jamie: Okay. What about lunch?

Jo: I'm afraid I [3]_____ with Andy.

Jamie: And the afternoon?

Jo: I [4]_____ with Andy and then I [5]_____ Sarah and Lisa in town.

Jamie: Dinner?

Jo: Sorry, but I [6]_____ at Grandpa's and then I [7]_____ to a party at Andy's.

Jamie: Oh well. Maybe another time .... By the way, who's Andy?

3 * Choose the correct words to complete the sentences.

1 Brad thinks he is overweight.
'(I'm going to lose)/I'm losing some weight.'

2 Ben is waiting outside a club with two tickets to see a rock band.
'I'm going to take/I'm taking Molly to see a gig.'

3 Jenny hasn't updated her Facebook page for a long time.
'I'm going to update/I'm updating my Facebook page this evening.'

4 Dennis has sent out all the invitations to his birthday party.
'I'm going to have/I'm having a party on Saturday.'

5 Debby is in the dentist's waiting room. She has an appointment 3 p.m.
'I'm going to see/I'm seeing the dentist at 3 p.m.'

6 Becky plays the guitar but can't read music.
'I'm going to learn/I'm learning how to read music one day.'

4 *** Use the cues to write sentences in the Present Simple.

1 **A:** The film / start / at 7.50 p.m.
B: What time / it finish?
A: *The film starts at 7.50 p.m.*
B: *What time does it finish?*

2 **A:** We / not have / an English lesson tomorrow
B: When / be / our next English lesson?
A: _____
B: _____

3 **A:** My flight / leave / Warsaw at 10.10 a.m.
B: What time / you arrive / in London?
A: _____
B: _____

4 **A:** The Post Office / close / at 4.30 p.m. today
B: What time / it open / tomorrow morning?
A: _____
B: _____

5 **A:** Liverpool / play / Manchester United this evening
B: Who / they play / next Saturday?
A: _____
B: _____

Grammar Alive Arrangements

5 ** Use the cues to write dialogues.

1 **A:** after school / go shopping
B: play tennis in a school competition
A: *Are you doing anything after school? We could go shopping.*
B: *I'm afraid I can't. I'm playing tennis in a school competition.*

2 **A:** this evening / meet up in town
B: look after my little brother and sister
A: _____
B: _____

3 **A:** for lunch / go to a café
B: have lunch with my family
A: _____
B: _____

4 **A:** Sunday / go for a bike ride
B: go to the beach with my girlfriend
A: _____
B: _____

5 **A:** Friday night / go to a club
B: work from 6 till 10 at the sports centre
A: _____
B: _____

33

SKILLS

Listening

➊ Complete the text with the words below.

cyber-bullying   homepage   keep in touch with
online   posted   view

I've stopped going on social networks now because
I was suffering from ¹*cyber-bullying*. Somebody was
posting aggressive comments on my homepage. I've
never ²_____ a nasty comment on anybody's
³_____, and I don't have any enemies so I think it
was a stranger. I don't like the idea that a stranger
can ⁴_____ my photos or my personal information.
Now, I prefer to ⁵_____ my friends by phone. If I
want my friends to see photos or videos, I don't need
to post them ⁶_____ I can send them on my phone.

➋ (2.29) Complete the sentences with one word. Listen and check.

1 ___Could___ I speak to Mrs Williams?
2 I'll _____ you through.
3 I'm _____ she's not available at the moment.
4 Could I leave her a _____?
5 _____ at all.

➌ (2.30) Listen to two phone conversations and correct the mistakes in the messages below.

Conversation A

> Your wife's *mother's* birthday tomorrow.
> Book restaurant for lunch for twelve
> people at 2.30.

Conversation B

> Can't meet for dinner tomorrow.
> Can you play tennis on Sunday? Amy
> will pick you up at two o'clock.

➍ Choose the correct expressions to complete the two conversations.

Conversation A

A: ¹___c___. Reception. Can I help you?
B: Yes, please. ²_____ Mr James, please? It's Amy.
A: Oh hello Amy. ³_____. ⁴_____.
B: Thanks.
A: ⁵_____ at the moment.
B: Oh, could I leave a message please?
A: Yes of course. Just a moment.
   (Amy leaves a message/the receptionist repeats it)
B: ⁶_____ _____
A: Not at all. Say happy birthday to your grandmother.

Conversation B

A: Hello.
B: ¹_____. Mrs Miles. It's Amy.
A: Oh, hello Amy.
B: ²_____ Matt, please?
A: Of course. ³_____. ⁴_____.
B: Thanks Mrs Miles.
A: ⁵_____. Do you want to leave a quick message.
(Amy leaves a message)
A: Okay, I'll tell him.
B: ⁶_____.

1 a Hi!
  b Hey!
  c Good morning.
2 a Can I speak to …
  b I want to speak to …
  c Could I speak to …
3 a Hold on a moment.
  b Hang on a sec.
  c Please wait.
4 a I'll get him for you.
  b I'll try.
  c I'll put you through.
5 a He's absent.
  b I'm afraid he's not available.
  c Sorry Amy, he's out.
6 a Thanks a lot.
  b Okay.
  c Thank you very much.

Check Your Progress 11

① **People** **Complete the description with the words below.**

> bit   hair   overweight   pale-skinned   shy   small   sociable   straight   characters

My sister and I are very different. I'm ¹_____ but my sister is tall. I've got curly blond ²_____ and my sister's got ³_____ brown hair. I think I'm quite like my mother - she's small but she isn't slim, she's a little ⁴_____. My sister is very ⁵_____ but my mother is quite dark-skinned. Our ⁶_____ are different too - my sister is confident, ⁷_____ and talkative, but I'm ⁸_____ and sensitive. Sometimes she's a ⁹_____ moody, but we are good ¹⁰_____.

/10

② ***get*** **Rewrite the underlined words or phrases with the correct form of *get*.**

> get rid of   don't get on well   get angry   get on with   get good marks

A: Do you <u>have a good relationship with</u> ¹_____ your sister.

B: Yes, usually. But sometimes we <u>don't have a good relationship</u> ²_____.

A: Oh, Why's that?

B: She always <u>achieves</u> good marks ³_____ at school.

A: What's wrong with that?

B: Well, I <u>become</u> angry ⁴_____ because she never helps me with my homework. Also, she had an annoying boyfriend but she <u>got</u> bored and <u>eliminated</u> ⁵_____ him.

/5

③ ***as* for comparisons** **Rewrite the sentences with the same meaning as the first one.**

1 Tanya is shorter than Emma. → Tanya isn't

_____

2 Tom and Dick are both hard-working. → Tom is

_____

3 Beth is more romantic that John. → John isn't

_____

4 Craig is untidy, just like his brother. → Craig's brother is just _____

5 My hair is curlier than yours. → Your hair isn't

_____

6 Alice is outgoing: the same as her mother. → Alice is _____

/6

④ **Intentions and arrangements** **Complete the sentences with the Present Continuous or *be going to* and the words in brackets. If both are possible, use the Present Continuous.**

1 He _____ at three o'clock this afternoon. (arrive)

2 I _____ her all my problems when I see her. (tell)

3 I _____ how to type one day. (learn)

4 We _____ back to Spain tomorrow morning. (fly)

5 _____ the phone? (you / answer)

6 They _____ us outside the cinema. (meet)

7 I _____ lunch with Sue today. (have)

8 We _____ Thailand one day. (visit)

/8

⑤ **Telephoning** **Put the conversation in order.**

A: No, thank you.

A: Thank you.

B: One moment. I'll put you through.

B: I'm afraid he's not available at the moment. Would you like to leave a message?

A: Good morning. Could I speak to Mr Young, please?

A: Goodbye.

/6

TOTAL SCORE **/35**

Module Diary 11

① **Look at the objectives on page 85 in the Students' Book. Choose three and evaluate your learning.**

1 Now I can _____
well / quite well / with problems.

2 Now I can _____
well / quite well / with problems.

3 Now I can _____
well / quite well / with problems.

② **Look at your results. What language areas in this module do you need to study more?**

Sound Choice 6

❶ **2.32** Grammar - *the* **Listen. Do you hear the /iː/ or /ə/? Put the geographical names in the correct column.**

~~Alps~~   Andes   Elbe   Himalayas   Indus
Nile   Rhine   Urals

/iː/ before vowel sounds
The ___*Alps*___
The _____
The _____
The _____
/ə/ before consonant sounds
The _____
The _____
The _____
The _____

❷ **2.33** Consonants /ŋ/ **Match the words to make noun phrases or adjectives. Then listen, check and repeat.**

1 cyber- _d_		**a** riding
2 easy- ___		**b** messaging
3 horse ___		**c** networking
4 instant ___		**d** bullying
5 social ___		**e** watching
6 whale ___		**f** going

❸ **2.34** Consonant clusters **Say the nouns. <u>Underline</u> the noun with a /z/ ending. Listen, check and repeat.**

1 crisps, dentists, paints, spring<u>s</u>
2 contests, friends, presidents, trips
3 coasts, islands, scientists, students

❹ **2.35** Vowels /ɜː/ and /ə/ **Listen and repeat the two-syllable words. Is /ə/ the stressed or the unstressed syllable?**

burner	earner
person	surfer
learner	further
urgent	worker

❺ **2.36** Spelling **Listen and complete the words in the chant with a vowel.**

Pearl's b_*u*_rn h____rts,
Kurt le____rns w____rds,
Earl's g____rl w____rks,
Bert's f____rst t____rm.

❻ **2.37** Difficult words **Put the three syllable words into the correct column. Then listen, check and repeat.**

addictive   canoeing   creator   ~~discipline~~   impatient
influence   sociable   tragedy

▇▪▪	▪▇▪
discipline	

TOPIC TALK – VOCABULARY

❶ Choose the correct six adjectives to match the pictures.

~~confusing~~ annoying exciting interesting
surprising boring in

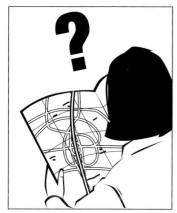

1 *confusing*

2 _____

3 _____

4 _____

5 _____

6 _____

❷ Describe the pictures by completing the sentences with appropriate adjectives from Exercise 2.

Picture 1 The map is *confusing*. The woman is *confused*.

Picture 2 The race is _____. The people are _____.

Picture 3 The dog is _____. The man is _____.

Picture 4 The lesson is _____. The students are _____.

Picture 5 The boy is _____. The exam result is _____.

Picture 6 The students are _____. The teacher is _____.

❸ <u>Underline</u> the word with the opposite meaning.

1 calm happy relaxed <u>upset</u>
2 angry annoyed happy irritated
3 scared calm shocked terrified
4 nervous relaxed stressed out worried

❹ Complete the text with the words below.

doing hobbies ~~mood~~ on with (x 2) get (x 2)

I'm a happy person and I'm usually in a good
¹*mood*. When I'm ²_____ my friends, I feel
enthusiastic about everything, but when I'm
³_____ my own, I sometimes ⁴_____ a bit
down. I find arguments ⁵_____ people really
stressful and upsetting. I like school, but I don't
like ⁶_____ tests and exams – I sometimes
⁷_____ a bit stressed. My favourite ⁸_____
are dancing and singing – they're relaxing and
exciting at the same time!

❺ Complete the sentence about yourself.

1 I'm usually _____
2 When I _____
3 I find _____
4 Doing _____
5 I'm interested _____
6 I'm bored _____

34

GRAMMAR
Defining relative clauses

REMEMBER

Complete exercises A–B before you start this lesson

A Underline the correct preposition.

1 Who's that boy *with/from/for* the book in his hand?
2 That's me, right *in/at/on* the back of the photo.
3 I'm meeting my friends *at/on/out* the cinema.
4 I've got lots of friends *on/at/in* my class.
5 Where are you going *for/in/on* holiday?
6 I've got a map *to/of/in* the island here.
7 I'd like a pizza *for/to/in* lunch today.
8 Our hotel is *in/on/at* the middle of the island.

B Complete the dialogue with the correct prepositions.

at (x 2)   in (x 2)   ~~of~~   on   with (x 3)

A: So who are these people?
B: They're a group ¹___*of*___ friends ²_____ the language school ³_____ Brighton.
A: Were they studying English with you?
B: Yes, that's right. The man ⁴_____ sunglasses was our teacher.
A: Wow, he looks young. Were all the students from Poland?
B: No ... the girl ⁵_____ short, dyed hair is German. The other girl ⁶_____ jeans is from Russia and the boy ⁷_____ the end is French.
A: Who's the boy ⁸_____ the back?
B: Which one?
A: The one ⁹_____ long, dark curly hair.
B: Oh that's Carlo, an Italian.
A: He's cute.
B: Yes, I know. He's coming to see me next week!
A: Really?!

1 * Underline the correct relative pronoun. Then match the answers below to the correct sentences.

a comedian   a psychologist   a spa   ~~stress~~
winter   yoga

1 An emotion *which/who* makes you feel nervous and worried. _*stress*_
2 A doctor *which/who* studies the mind to try and explain human behaviour. _____
3 A type of exercise *where/that* keeps you fit and relaxes your mind. _____
4 A place *where/which* people go to relax and improve their health. _____
5 A time of year *when/where* many people get a bit depressed. _____
6 An entertainer *who/which* tries to make you laugh. _____

2 * Match the sentence beginnings (1–8) with the sentence endings (a–h).

1 Tom is a man _d_
2 Greece is the country ___
3 Friday afternoon is the time ___
4 Crying is something ___
5 That's the woman ___
6 Childhood is a time ___
7 My parents are watching a film ___
8 I'm going to a place ___

a when I feel most relaxed.
b which I never do.
c where I'd like to live.
d who I respect.
e that was made in 1935.
f where I can concentrate.
g who shouted at us.
h when there is nothing to worry about.

3 ** Underline relative clauses and cross out pronouns where possible.

1 The book ~~that~~ I'm reading is very interesting.
2 My best friend is the only person who understands me.
3 I've got a cousin who gets upset very easily.
4 Global warming is the issue which I worry about most.
5 I don't like watching films that make me cry.
6 Doing exams is the thing that I hate most about school.

4 *** Complete the text with the relative pronouns at the end of each line.

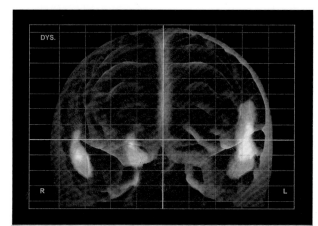

In the mood?

Do you have friends *who* are always   ~~who~~
in a bad mood? Scientists now believe
that moods may begin in an area of the
brain important things like your heart   where
rate and your breathing are controlled.
In recent experiments, the researchers
measured brain activity at a time their   when
student volunteers were feeling down.
The students were in a particularly bad   who
mood had extra blood flowing to this
part of the brain. The psychologist led   who
the experiment hopes that the new
information will be useful. 'It may help
us to find better ways of treating the
millions have problems with depression   who
each year,' he said.

5 *** Join the sentences to make one sentence with a relative pronoun.

1 I was talking to some friends. They were all stressed out.
I was talking to some friends who
were all stressed out.

2 There's a great beach in Egypt. We go snorkelling there. _____

3 I read a different magazine. It was better than this one. _____

4 My friend was really good to me. I was depressed.
_____

5 I was terrified. I saw the exam questions.
_____

6 I know a good café. I go there to meet my friends.
_____

7 I saw a film yesterday. It was really boring.
_____

8 I've just seen a man. He was crying.
_____

Grammar Alive Descriptions

6 * Complete the survey questions with a relative pronoun.

Do you feel good when you …

1 watch films __which/that__ have happy endings?

2 remember a time _____ you were very happy?

3 see a baby _____ smiles at you?

4 remember a place _____ you had a good holiday?

5 help a friend _____ has a problem?

6 hear a joke _____ makes you laugh?

7 ** Use the cues to write sentences about *Slumdog Millionaire*.

1 it / film / win / eight Oscars / 2009
It is a film which won eight Oscars in 2009.

2 it / about / a young man / appear on *Who wants to be a millionaire.*
_____

3 A 'slumdog' / person / be / someone / very poor
_____

4 Telluride, Colorado / place / the film / be first shown
_____

5 30 August 2008 / date / the film / be first shown
_____

6 A.R. Rahman / man / wrote / the music for the film
_____

1 **2.38** **Listen to three conversations. Match the information (a-c) to the correct situations (1-3).**

1 Where is the dialogue taking place?
a at a party _2_   **b** at home ___
c in a school ___

2 Who is speaking in each of the dialogues?
a two friends ___
b a father and a teacher ___
c a mother and a son ___

3 In which dialogue does somebody feel ...
a confused? ___   **b** worried? ___
c nervous? ___

4 In which dialogue does somebody ...
a ask for advice? ___   **b** ask for an opinion? ___
c ask somebody to do something? ___

Word Builder *make* and *do*

2 **Choose the correct words to complete the sentences about the conversations.**

1 Toby is going to *do*/make some exercise to relax. _T_
2 His mother wants him to *do/make* something for her. ___
3 Julie has *done/made* a decision about Tom. ___
4 Julie's friend thinks she should *do/make* a list of Tom's good and bad qualities. ___
5 Mr Jones thinks Oliver is *doing/making* an effort at school. ___
6 Oliver's teacher thinks he's *doing/making* well at school. ___

3 **2.38** **Which sentences in Exercise 2 are true (T) or false (F)? Listen again and check.**

Sentence Builder *too/not* enough

4 **Complete the texts with *too* or *not enough* and the adjective in brackets.**

What makes **you happy?**
Share your tips.

1 Life is ¹___too___ (short) to be unhappy. I'm ²_____ (rich) to buy expensive clothes or to go out every night. But it doesn't matter. You can't buy happiness. Simple things make me happy – chocolate, sunshine, my cat.

Sarah

2 Most people are ³_____ (serious). Life is for laughing and smiling. It works for me when I'm feeling down.
Tim

3 Of course family and friends are the most important things in my life, but sleeping is great. When I sleep well I feel relaxed about life and happy ... I love it! When I feel ⁴_____ (stressed out), I don't sleep well.

Andrew

4 It's easy to get depressed when you have negative thoughts. People are always thinking, 'I'm ⁵_____ (fat), I'm ⁶_____ (clever), I'm ⁷_____ (rich), I'm ⁸_____ (ugly).' You need to try to think positively and good things will happen.

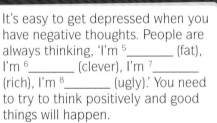
Amy

5 Every time I go surfing, I feel happy. Nice weather and a good group of friends is all I need to stay happy. Some of my friends say they're ⁹_____ (busy) to have a hobby, but if they tried they would see that it makes a big difference to how you feel.

Zac

5 **Match the tips (a-e) for being happy with the paragraphs (1-5) in the text.**

a Find a hobby you love. _5_
b Enjoy the simple things in life. ___
c Try going to bed earlier. ___
d Learn to like yourself as you are. ___
e Be a little crazy from time to time. ___

LESSON 36

GRAMMAR
Reporting advice, orders and requests

❶ * Rewrite the reported sentences as direct speech.

1 Rupert told me to send him an email. '
   Send me an email. '
2 Vicky told me to call her next week.
   'Call _____.'
3 Ted advised me to ask my father.
   'Why _____?'
4 Sally asked me to help her.
   'Can _____?
5 Wendy told me not to come.
   'Don't _____.'
6 Flo told me not to worry but to be happy.
   'Don't _____.'

❷ ** Choose the correct words to complete the sentences.

1 'Could you please open the window.' He asked/
   advised me to open the window.
2 'I really hope you can come.' She really wanted/told
   me to come.
3 'Please don't forget your keys.' He ordered/told me
   not to forget my keys.
4 'Leave early if you can.' They asked/advised us to
   leave early.
5 'Get up this minute!' My mum advised/ordered me
   to get up.
6 'Please don't tell anyone.' She asked/advised him
   not to tell anyone.

❸ ** Complete the sentences with reported speech.

1 'Be careful.' Mum told _me to be careful_.
2 'Don't interrupt me.'
   My dad told _____.
3 'Why don't you call her and explain the problem.'
   My friend advised _____.
4 'Can you wait a bit longer?'
   My sister asked _____.
5 'Show me your identity card now!' The policeman
   ordered _____.
6 'I'd really like you to stay.'
   My friend wanted _____.
7 'Don't come home late.'
   Dad told _____.
8 'Could you help me with my homework?' My sister
   asked _____.

❹ ** Write reported sentences with the verb in brackets.

1 Tim: 'Peter, can you look after my bag?' (ask)
   Tim asked Peter to look after his bag.
2 Mike: 'Sue, why don't you wait for a bit' (advise)
   _____
3 Jenny's dad: 'Jenny, go up to your room. Now!'
   (order)
   _____
4 Viv: 'Gina, would you lend me some money.' (want)
   _____
5 Jane: 'Joe, don't talk to strangers.' (tell)
   _____
6 Gary: 'Liz, please don't tell Neil about Sarah.' (ask)
   _____

❺ *** Read the Top tips for a happy life and complete the sentences (1-6).

Top tips for a happy life
- Always look on the bright side of life. Don't think negatively. Think positively.
- Think of solutions, not problems.
- Always look at what you have done. Don't look at what you haven't done.
- Each day do something good: do at least one thing to make somebody else happy.
- Mix with happy people – it helps.
- Smile more!

1 The speaker told us
   to look on the bright side. He told us not
   to think negatively but to think positively.
2 He asked us
   _____
   _____
3 He advised us
   _____
   _____
4 He told us
   _____
   _____
5 He advised us
   _____
   _____
6 Finally, he told us
   _____
   _____

Workshop 6

Writing

1 Match the formal language in the note with the informal language below.

a Maybe she's _2_ **d** to have a chat about it ___
b Thanks a lot. ___ **e** Give me a ring ___
c A quick note ___ **f** We can ___

> Hi Polly
>
> ¹I am writing to you to ask you something. I've just spoken to Julie and she sounds angry. ²I think she might be annoyed with me, but I don't know why. Can we meet ³to discuss the problem? ⁴I suggest we meet up after school. ⁵Telephone me at home.
>
> ⁶Thank you very much,
>
> Grace

Sentence Builder Purpose linkers

2 Use the cues to write requests and suggestions.

1 meet up at 6.p.m. / do our homework together (so that)

Can we meet up at 6.p.m. so that we can do
our homework together?

2 meet up after school / have a good chat (to)

_____

3 borrow your bicycle / get to my piano lesson on time (so that)

_____

4 call you later / get directions to the party (to)

_____

3 Read the reply and complete the message. Ask your friend a favour, suggest where to meet and how to contact you.

Message

> You know I'm going to my cousin's wedding next weekend? Well, I'm really excited about it, but _____ _____ _____ _____ _____

Reply

> Sorry, I can't meet on Friday – I've got a basketball match. Is Saturday okay? I can meet you in town so that we can go to the shopping centre. There are loads of good clothes shops there.

Speaking

1 Match the statements (1-5) with the correct responses (a-e).

1 I went to a Shakira concert on Saturday. _c_
2 I'm taking part in a debate about climate change next week. ___
3 I go horseriding every weekend. ___
4 Jane was in Paris recently. ___
5 I've won a writing competition. ___

a Do you? That's great.
b Was she? Brilliant!
c Did you? Lucky you!
d Have you? Congratulations.
e Are you? That sounds interesting.

2 (2.39) Complete the dialogue with tag questions. Then listen and check.

A: Hi. How was your weekend?
B: Great. I went to an opera.
A: ¹_Did you_? Are you joking? I thought you hated classical music.
B: Well, I decided to do something different. I went with my parents. The tickets cost fifty euros each.
A: ²_____ they? That's crazy.
B: I know and I had to wear an evening dress.
A: ³_____you? I don't believe it!
B: But it was a great experience.
A: ⁴_____ it?
B: Yes, the main singers were amazing.
A: ⁵_____ they? But it's opera …
B: I know, but I really enjoyed it.
A: ⁶_____ you?
B: Yes, and the main singer was really good-looking. He looked like George Clooney.
A: ⁷_____ he?
B: Yes – and he had a fantastic voice. I'm definitely going to go to the opera again.
A: ⁸_____ you? I don't think I'll come with you – it's too expensive!

Check Your Progress 12

1 Feelings *-ed* and *-ing* Complete the sentences with the same meaning as the one above.

1 I'm very relaxed at weekends.
   I find weekends are _____.
2 Thinking about the future is very depressing.
   I get _____ thinking about the future.
3 When I go to see live music I always feel excited.
   Seeing live music is _____.
4 The lesson today was really boring.
   I was _____ in the lesson today.
5 I found the instructions for my new phone were very confusing.
   I was very _____ by the instructions for my new phone.
6 Meeting new people is always very interesting.
   I'm always _____ in meeting new people.

/6

2 Defining relative clauses Complete the sentences with the words in brackets and the correct relative pronoun.

1 The book is very interesting. (I am reading it.)
   The book _____ is very interesting.
2 The town is very depressing. (I was born there.)
   The town _____ is very depressing.
3 Summer is a season. (People feel relaxed.)
   Summer is a season _____
4 Claire was a girlfriend. (She broke my heart.)
   Claire was the girlfriend _____
5 She's found the keys. (She lost them.)
   She's found the keys _____
6 They are the students. (I met them yesterday.)
   They are the students _____

/6

3 *make* and *do* Complete the questions with the correct form of *make* or *do*.

1 Have you _____ any exercise this week?
2 What _____ you angry?
3 Could you _____ a list of things to buy?
4 Do you think it will _____ a difference?
5 Is he _____ well at school?
6 Why can't you _____ a decision?
7 I think you could _____ better.
8 She _____ an effort to work harder.
9 The present _____ her happy.

/9

4 *not enough/too* Complete the sentences with the same meaning as the one above. Use *not enough* or *too*.

1 This T-shirt isn't big enough. _____
2 You're too young to watch that film. _____
3 It isn't warm enough to play outside. _____
4 She's too nervous to do well in exams. _____
5 This soup isn't cool enough to eat yet. _____
6 These exercises are too easy for our students.
   _____
7 The TV is too small. _____
8 These shoes aren't big enough. _____

/8

5 Reporting advice, orders and requests Complete the sentences with reported advice about James going to university.

1 'Work hard.'
   His granddad told _____
2 'Don't go to too many parties.'
   His mum told _____
3 'Text or call me every day.'
   His girlfriend asked _____
4 'Be careful with your money.'
   His dad told _____
5 'Don't stay in bed all day.'
   His mum told _____
6 'Have a great time!'
   His parents want _____

/6

TOTAL SCORE   /35

Module Diary 12

1 Look at the objectives on page 93 in the Students' Book. Choose three and evaluate your learning.

1 Now I can _____
   well / quite well / with problems.
2 Now I can _____
   well / quite well / with problems.
3 Now I can _____
   well / quite well / with problems.

2 Look at your results. What language areas in this module do you need to study more?

Exam Choice 6

Reading

1 Read the text and answer the questions.

  1 Where would you find this description of Laughter Yoga classes?

    a in a newspaper **b** on a website **c** in a brochure

  2 Who is the text written for?

    a children **b** old people **c** adults

  3 What is the purpose of the text?

    a to compare Laughter Yoga with ordinary yoga

    b to tell the history of Laughter Yoga

    c to advertise Laughter Yoga classes

Home	About us	Classes	Business laughter	Contact us

Discover how laughter can work for you!

You've probably heard the expression 'Laughter is the best medicine'. Well, scientists and medical doctors now agree that laughter can help people to deal with stress and anger. Research has shown that people who feel happy and relaxed are healthier and have better relationships.

What is laughter yoga?

Laughter Yoga is a series of exercises. Laughter Yoga teaches you to laugh for no reason. You don't have to have a sense of humour, or understand funny jokes. You just have to laugh.

When you do Laughter Yoga in a group, you laugh and do yoga breathing, so that you increase the amount of oxygen in your body. Soon the laughter exercises turn into real laughter. After a laughter yoga class, you feel calm and relaxed, but also full of energy and happy.

Click **here** to watch a video

Where does Laughter Yoga come from?

Laughter Yoga was developed by Dr Kataria, a doctor from India. Laughter Yoga classes started in a park in Mumbai in 1995 with just five people, and now there are over 6,000 laughter clubs in sixty different countries.

Julie Whitehead was one of the first people in the UK to become a Laughter Yoga teacher with Dr Kataria. She says, 'yoga has been a part of my life for thirty years, but in 2002 my life changed when I discovered Laughter Yoga. I am particularly interested in health and well-being.'

She is a member of Laughter Network, a group of professionals who want to bring more laughter, health and happiness into people's lives. They run Laughter Yoga classes and workshops in the UK, and Julie runs Laughter Yoga holidays in Turkey, Egypt, Spain and Morocco.

For more information click

What are the health benefits of Laughter Yoga?

Laughing is good for the body and the mind. When we laugh we breathe more oxygen into our body, which helps to keep us healthy. Endorphins, or happy chemicals, are released in the body, and you feel more relaxed and happy. Laughter also brings people together to share some fun.

Companies who have run laughter yoga workshops find that they have advantages for both employers and employees. People who are happy at work are more hard-working and make more money for the company. Also, people who can laugh together, communicate more successfully. In general, people do better at work when they feel happy and relaxed.

A Danish company who used Laughter Yoga for a year reported an increase in sales of 40 percent over the previous year. Following Laughter Yoga session, a Hawaiian timeshare company reported the highest sales of the year - double their target figures.

If you're not sure about Laughter Yoga, remember this, children laugh 300–400 times a day, but adults only laugh around fifteen times a day.

Get more laughter in your life - you can feel the change in you, and when you change, the world changes. Laughter really is the best medicine.

Click **here** to read what people say about Laughter Yoga

2 **Read the text again and answer the questions.**

1 Why is it good to laugh and do yoga breathing exercises at the same time?
2 Where and when did Laughter Yoga classes begin?
3 How long has Julie Whitehead been doing Laughter Yoga?
4 What does Laughter Network want to do?
5 What are the advantages for a company when their employees do laughter yoga?

Listening

3 **2.40** **Listen to three conversations. Match the information (a–c) to the correct situations (1–3).**

1 Where is the dialogue taking place?
  a doctor's surgery ___
  b in a supermarket ___
  c on the phone ___
2 Who is speaking in each of the three dialogues?
  a doctor/patient ___
  b mother/son's friend ___
  c two friends ___
3 What time of day is it?
  a evening ___
  b afternoon ___
  c morning ___
4 In which dialogue does somebody ...
  a make a request? ___
  b give advice? ___
  c ask for a suggestion? ___

Speaking

4 **2.41** **Listen to a dialogue. Are the sentences true (T) or false (F)?**

1 Meg was in a dance competition at the weekend. ___
2 She didn't win anything. ___
3 She danced hip hop. ___
4 Her parents went with her. ___
5 She was too shy to speak to any famous people. ___

5 **2.41** **Complete the extracts from the dialogue. Listen again and check.**

Meg I took part in a dance competition on Saturday evening, and I won!
Alex ¹_____ you? Congratulations. That's great news.
Meg I was really nervous. In fact, I was terrified!
Alex ²_____ you?
Meg There were some famous people there, too.
Alex ³_____? Who?
Meg Shakira was there.
Alex ⁴_____? Wow. Why was she there?
Meg Well, it was a charity dance competition, and she does a lot of work for charity.
Alex Oh, ⁵_____ she? Did she sing?

Exam Choice 6

Use of English

6 Complete the text with the correct form of the words in capitals.

When looking for a friend, what is the most important thing for you? Do you want someone who is ¹_____ or is it more important that he, or she, has a nice ²_____?	ATTRACT PERSON
We asked a number of teenagers for their opinions and this is what we found out. Most teenagers have friends who are similar to them. They have the same ³_____, which isn't surprising since most of us make friends at school. They also	EDUCATE
choose friends whose ⁴_____ is similar. Well-behaved children like other well-behaved children. Interests are also	BEHAVE
important. ⁵_____ teenagers often like other teenagers who take an active interest in or who are ⁶_____ about sports and keeping fit.	SPORT ENTHUSIASM
What about different kinds of ⁷_____, not friends but boy/girl friends? Most girls we asked liked their boyfriends to	RELATION
be ⁸_____ and to make them laugh but they also wanted them to be thoughtful, kind and, of course, ⁹_____. Most of them told us that, when they had an ¹⁰_____ with their boyfriends, it was usually because the boys had forgotten something important like a birthday or a date. What about boys … ?	FUN ROMANCE ARGUE

Writing

7 Complete the short notes with the words in the box.

as (x 2)   not as (x 2)   so that (x 3)   to (x 2)

Hi Tom

A quick note ¹_____ ask you something. I'm going to have a party ²_____ celebrate the end of exams. But I'm ³_____ organised ⁴_____ you. Can you help me? Is five o'clock tomorrow okay? I can cycle to your house ⁵_____ you don't have to come out. Text me.

All the best, Lou

Hi Lou

No problem, but why don't we meet up in town ⁶_____ you don't have to cycle too far. Is it okay if I bring my sister? I'm ⁷_____ organised ⁸_____ you think, but my sister's really helpful. Can you call me ⁹_____ we can decide the best place to meet in town?

COMPUTER GAMES

Task: Write a review of your favourite computer game
Tools: www.amazon.co.uk
Skills: Finding and selecting information

Before you start

1 Read the review of a video game. What does the reviewer tell you about the game? Order the comments below.

amazon.co.uk   Hello. Sign in to get personalised recommendations. New Customer? Start here.   Find the Hottest Summer Offers
Your Amazon.co.uk | Today's Deals | Gift Cards | Gifts & Wish Lists   Your Account | Help
Shop All Departments | Search | PC & Video Games | GO | Basket | Wish List
PC & Video Games | 3DS | DS | Wii | PS3 | Xbox 360 | PC & Mac | Bestsellers | Future Releases | Accessories | Bundles | Special Offers | Trade-In | Rental

By **SimsFan**
★★★☆

I love The Sims! It's a strategy game and you control the lives of cartoon characters – the 'Sims'. You help them work, play, shop and do things in their houses. I bought the first Sims when I was thirteen and I played it every day. This new version is much better – it has got amazing graphics, lots of new and fun characters and incredible music. But it does crash sometimes. ☹ It's not a cheap game (£19.99), but it is great fun!

Quantity: 1
Add to Basket
or
Sign in to turn on 1-Click ordering.
or
Add to Basket with FREE One-Day Delivery
Amazon Prime free trial required. Sign up when you check out. Learn more
Add to Wish List

💬 Comments (6)

a What happens in the game ___
b The kind of game ___
c The name of the game _1_
d What features it has ___
e The price ___
f Problems with the game ___

2 Answer the questions below about your favourite computer game.

1 What is the name of the game?
_____

2 What kind of game is it (role-playing, simulation)?
_____

3 What happens in the game (is there a story)?
_____

4 What features does it have (graphics, music, levels)?
_____

5 How much does it cost?
_____

6 Does it have any problems?
_____

7 Why do you like it?
_____

Research

3 Go to www.amazon.co.uk and search for your game.

Tip!
Sometimes the language in online reviews is difficult, so don't try to understand every word. Try to get a general idea of the review. If you don't understand a sentence, you can use an online translator like Google Translate, www.translate.google.com but remember that online translators are not a 100 percent accurate.

4 Read some of the reviews and make notes. Do not copy the text from the webpage.

What do people like about the game?
_____

What do people dislike about the game?
_____

Are there any problems with the game?
_____

Task

5 Use your answers from Exercise 2 and your notes from Exercise 4 to write a review of your favourite computer game. Use the model from Exercise 1 to help you.

6 Give your review to the other students in your class to read. Which computer game do most of the class like best?

Review
In this task I have:
• found out information about computer games on the internet and used it to write a review.

STORIES

Task: Research teen books and find one to read
Tools: www.bestbooks4teens.com
Skills: Finding specific information on one website

Before you start

❶ **Think about your reading habits. Answer the questions.**

1 What kinds of books do you like? Do you like science fiction, romance, crime, horror, fantasy, action or adventure books?
2 What's the best book you have read?
3 What's the worst book you have read?

❷ **Read the description of a book. Answer the questions.**

"John Stone is just a quiet history teacher until the day he discovers an old book in a box at the back of his classroom. The book tells the story of <u>treasure</u> hidden in the mountains in Peru. Inside the book there is an old map. Stone takes the map and travels to Peru to find the treasure. But other people are also looking for the treasure - dangerous people who will do anything to find it. Stone travels from the mountains of Peru to the forests of Russia, to find the treasure and bring it home to the national museum."

1 What type of book is it?

_____

2 How do you know this? <u>Underline</u> the words that helped you decide.

3 Do you think this book is interesting? Why / Why not?

_____

Research

❸ **Go to www.bestbooks4teens.com and find a book to read.**

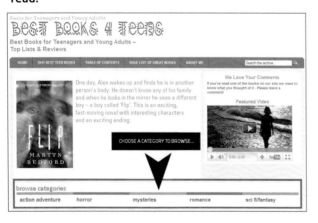

Tip!

When you use the search box on a website, you do not need to type in complete sentences or questions, or add punctuation. You can just type the key words.

❹ **Use the headings below to make notes about the book you choose.**

Book title: _____

Type of book: _____

Story: _____

_____

Three plot keywords: _____

_____

Why you like it: _____

_____

Task

❺ **Use your notes from Exercise 4 to write a short description of the book. Say why you like the book and want to read it. Use the description from Exercise 3 to help you.**

❻ **Give your description to the other students in your class to read. Which book do most of the class want to read?**

Review

In this task I have:
• researched books and written a short description to share with the class.

FESTIVALS

Task: Find out about music festivals in the UK
Tools: www.downloadfestival.co.uk www.vfestival.com
Skills: Finding specific information online

Before you start

1 Think about the music you like. Answer the questions.

1 What kind of music do you like? Do you like pop, rock, reggae or rap?
2 Who are your favourite singers or groups?
3 Have you ever been to a music festival or concert?

Research

2 Go to the two festival websites below, and complete the table.

- Download Festival - **www.downloadfestival.co.uk**
- V Festival - **www.vfestival.com**

	Download Festival	V Festival
Type of music (folk / rock & pop / heavy metal / jazz …)		
Where is it?		
Dates for this year		
Ticket prices		
Two main singers or groups		
Camping facilities?		
Two things to bring		

Tip!
To find out who is playing at the festival click on 'line-up'. If there are no dates or singers for this year, look at last year's festival. Follow links to 'tickets' to find prices for the festival.

Task

3 Choose one of the two festivals from Exercise 2. Use the information you found to write a short paragraph about it. Use the example below to help you.

> I want to go to the V festival because it's got good music and it isn't too expensive. The festival takes place in Weston Park in the UK, in August, and tickets cost £120. Two important singers/ groups are Arctic Monkeys and Rihanna. You can camp there. Two things you should bring are your ticket and ID. You can't bring pets.

4 Give your paragraph to another student in your class to read. Which festival do most of the class want to go to?

Review
In this task I have:
- researched music festivals and written a paragraph with the information I found.

ENDANGERED ANIMALS

Task: Find out about endangered animals
Tools: www.life.com www.worldwildlife.org
Skills: Evaluating online sources

Before you start

1 **What do you know about endangered animals? Put the words below in the correct column of the table.**

gorilla bear rhino shark turtle
toad leopard alligator ~~tiger~~ bee

Endangered	Not endangered
tiger	

Research

2 Go to www.life.com/gallery/23283/critically-endangered-creatures#index/0 and check your answers to Exercise 1.

3 Look carefully at the website *around* the slides of endangered animals. Answer the questions.

1 Is it easy to find the Home page of this website?

_____

2 What other information is on the website? (Look at the tabs across the top.)

_____

3 Can you search for things on the website?

_____

4 Is this page up to date? When was this page made? (Look at the bottom of the page.)

_____

5 Is this page a reliable source?

_____

Tip!
When you are on the internet, think about these things:
- Is the website a personal website, or from an organisation?
- What other information is on the website? Is it reliable?
- How much advertising is on the website?
- What does the url (web address) tell you about the page?
- Is the website regularly updated?

To check if the information is correct, you should compare it with other websites.

4 **Go to www.worldwildlife.org and look carefully at the website. Answer the checklist of questions from the tip box.**

5 **Click on the 'Species' tab and choose one of the animals from the list. Use the headings below to make notes about the animal you choose.**

Name: _____

Lives in: _____

Colour: _____

Dangerous? _____

How many left? _____

Endangered? _____

Other interesting fact: _____

_____

Task

6 **Use your notes from Exercise 5 to write a short paragraph of forty to fifty words about your animal. Don't put the name of your animal in your paragraph.**

7 **Give your paragraph to the other students in your class to read. Can they guess the name of your animal?**

Review
In this task I have:
- learnt about endangered animals and about how to evaluate digital sources,
- written a paragraph about an animal.

HOLIDAYS

Task: Read online reviews of unusual hotels and choose one to stay in
Tools: www.tripadvisor.com
Skills: Evaluating online customer reviews

Before you start

1 Where do you think these three unusual hotels are? Write a country from below next to each hotel.

Sweden   Kenya   Canada

1 Hotel de Glase
At this hotel you sleep in an ice room. _____

2 The Giraffe Manor
At this hotel you can feed giraffes from your window. _____

3 Utter Inn
At this hotel your room is under a lake. _____

2 Go to http://listverse.com/2010/11/05/top-10-unusual-hotels/ and check your answers to Exercise 1.

3 Imagine you are going to stay in the Hotel de Glase *or* The Giraffe Manor. What is important for you when choosing a hotel? Put this list in order of importance.

Location ___   Activities ___   Food ___
Price ___   Things to see ___
Rooms ___   Things to do ___

Research

4 Go to www.tripadvisor.com and type 'Hotel de Glase' in the search box.

☺☺ tripadvisor.co.uk   The world's largest travel review site

Read five reviews. Write some positive and negative comments from the reviews. Then type 'The Giraffe Manor' in the search box and do the same as you did for Hotel de Glase.

Tip!
It's a good idea to read a lot of customer reviews before you make a decision, because people can have very different opinions of the same thing!

Task

5 Decide which of the two hotels you want to stay in. Use the cues below to write a short paragraph explaining your choice.

I like _____ hotel because
_____
_____.

The rooms are _____ and there are lots of things to do, like _____
_____
_____.

Review
In this task I have:
• read customer reviews and used the information to choose a hotel to visit.

EMOTIONS AND FILMS

Task: Watch trailers for two films from Students' Book page 93, and write about how they make you feel

Tools: www.trailers.apple.com www.imdb.com

Skills: Searching for online video via multiple sources and evaluating the differences

Before you start

1 Think of a film that made you feel happy, sad or excited.

Research

2 Watch the official trailer for *Slumdog Millionaire* and *(500) Days of Summer* on the websites below.

- iTunes movie trailers: **http://trailers.apple.com**
- The Internet movie database (IMDb): **http://imdb.com**

3 How do the two film trailers make you feel? Write three sentences about *Slumdog Millionaire* and *(500) Days of Summer*.

Slumdog Millionaire is a depressing film because
the hero is very poor.
Slumdog Millionaire is also an amusing film because ...

_____

_____

_____

4 Look again at the two film trailer websites. They are different. On which site can you:

1 see only the official film trailer?

_____

2 see more information about the film?

_____

3 buy the film online?

_____

4 link to articles about the film?

_____

5 see a customer review rating, with stars?

_____

6 see a link to the official film site?

_____

7 read quotes from the movie?

_____

8 write a review of the movie?

_____

Tip!

When you want to search for video on the internet, there are many different websites you can look at. To get extra information look at more than one website.

Task

5 Choose a film you want to see. Watch the trailer and complete the review below.

> Title: _____
>
> The acting is ... (good/poor/great) _____
>
> The photography is ...
>
> _____
>
> The special effects are ...
>
> _____
>
> In conclusion, the film looks ...
> (interesting/exciting/boring)
>
> _____

6 Give your review to the other students in your class to read. Which film do most of the class like best?

Review

In this task I have:

- **looked at two film trailers on two websites and evaluated the differences,**
- **written a short film review.**

Topic Wordlist

COUNTRY AND SOCIETY

crime and law
arrest (v)
body (n)
cell (n)
exile (n)
guard (n)
judge (n)
massacre (n)
prison (n)
prisoner (n)
punishment (n)

politics
autocracy (n)
communist (adj)
democracy (n)
democratic (adj)
dictator (n)
emperor (n)
government (n)
protest (n)
revolution (n)
war (n)

CULTURE

cultural events
arena (n)
audience (n)
book (v)
celebration (n)
concert (n)
film premiere (n)
parade (n)
St Patrick's Day (n)
ticket (n)

describing films/books
be about (v)
bestseller (n)
boring (adj)
brilliant (adj)
depressing (adj)
exciting (adj)
favourite (adj)
funny (adj)
imaginative (adj)
interesting (adj)
romantic (adj)
sad (adj)

scary (adj)
take place (v)
violent (adj)

literature
adventure story (n)
classic (n)
comedy (n)
cowboy story (n)
crime story (n)
detective story (n)
fairy tale (n)
fantasy story (n)
folk story (n)
ghost story (n)
historical story (n)
horror story (n)
love story (n)
romance (n)
science fiction story (n)
short story (n)
thriller (n)

music
album (n)
band (n)
catchy (adj)
CD (n)
choir (n)
group (n)
musician (n)
orchestra (n)
perform (v)
singer (n)
song (n)
track (n)
tribute band (n)
vinyl (n)
volume (n)

musical instruments
bagpipes (n)
cello (n)
clarinet (n)
drums (n)
flute (n)
guitar (n)
harp (n)
piano (n)
saxophone (n)
trumpet (n)
violin (n)

television and film
autograph (n)
comedian (n)

fan (n)
horror (adj)
reality show (n)
review (n)
sci-fi (adj)
silent-film (n)

theatre
audition (n)
box office (n)
stage (n)
street performer (n)

types of music
blues (adj)
classical (adj)
country and western (adj)
dance (adj)
folk (adj)
heavy metal (adj)
hip hop (adj)
indie (adj)
jazz (adj)
new age (adj)
pop (adj)
punk (adj)
rap (adj)
rock (adj)
soul (adj)
world (adj)

FAMILY AND SOCIAL LIFE

daily routine
do homework (v)
do jobs in the house (v)
get up (v)
go to bed (v)
shower (v)
sleep (v)

family
aunt (n)
brother (n)
cousin (n)
father/mother-in-law (n)
grandparent (n)
half-brother/sister (n)
nephew (n)
niece (n)
parent (n)
stepfather/mother (n)
uncle (n)

leisure time

acting (n)
air guitar (n)
board game (n)
celebrate (v)
chess (n)
cinema (n)
collecting coins (n)
collecting stamps (n)
costume (n)
dancing (n)
discotheque (n)
fancy-dress (n)
free running (n)
invitiation (n)
making jewellery (n)
making model aeroplanes (n)
Messenger (n)
music DVDs (n)
party (n)
photography (n)
pocket money (n)
singing (n)
spend time (v)

relationships

argue (v)
ask somebody out (v)
couple (n)
date (n)
fall in love (v)
generation gap (n)
get engaged (v)
get married (v)
get on okay with (v)
get on well (v)
get on well with (v)
go out with (v)
honeymoon (n)
love at first sight (n)
meet (v)

FOOD

describing food and drink

crisps (n)
drink (n)
fast food (n)
food items
fish (n)
fruit (n)
herb (n)
honey (n)
meat (n)
potato salad (n)

poultry (n)
ready-made (adj)
seafood (n)
soft drink (n)
spaghetti bolognese (n)
spice (n)
sweet (n)
turkey (n)
unhealthy (adj)
vegetable (n)
vegetarian (adj)

HEALTH

healthcare and treatment

Accident and Emergency (n)
ambulance (n)
amputate (v)
antibiotic (n)
drug (n)
emergency call (n)
first aid (n)
hospital (n)
injection (n)
laser (n)
medicine (n)
operation (n)
painkiller (n)
patient (n)
pill (n)
protect (v)
remedy (n)
tablet (n)
treatment (n)
vaccine (n)
X-ray (n)

healthy/unhealthy lifestyle

diet (n)
do exercise (v)
exercise (n)
fit (adj)
healthy (adj)
meditation (n)
physical exercise (n)
smoke (v)
stress (n)
unhealthy (adj)
well-being (n)

illness/injury

accident (n)
AIDS (n)
allergy (n)
asthma (n)

bacteria (n)
bleed (v)
breathing problems (n)
bug (n)
cold (n)
cough (n)
diabetes (n)
diarrhoea (n)
disease (n)
earache (n)
epidemic (n)
faint (adj)
flu (n)
germ (n)
get over (v)
hayfever (n)
headache (n)
hurt (v)
infection (n)
infectious (adj)
injure (v)
malaria (n)
obesity (n)
pain (n)
sick (adj)
sore throat (n)
sting (v)
stomachache (n)
sun cream (n)
sunburn (n)
swollen (adj)
temperature (n)
toothache (n)
tuberculosis (n)
unconscious (adj)
virus (n)
vomit (v)

NATURAL ENVIRONMENT

animals

alligator (n)
bat (n)
bear (n)
bee (n)
bird (n)
bull (n)
butterfly (n)
deer (n)
fox (n)
hippo (n)
insect (n)
lion (n)

lizard (n)
mammal (n)
monkey (n)
mosquito (n)
puma (n)
rat (n)
reptile (n)
scorpion (n)
shark (n)
snake (n)
species (n)
spider (n)
tiger (n)
toad (n)
wasp (n)
whale (n)
wolf (n)
worm (n)

climate
climate (n)
cool (adj)
storm (n)
sunny (adj)
tropical (adj)
windy (adj)

environmental issues
air pollution (n)
climate change (n)
destroy (v)
ecologist (n)
endangered (n)
habitat loss (n)
noise (n)
over-fishing (n)
over-hunting (n)
poisonous (adj)
pollution (n)
traffic (n)
water pollution (n)

landscape
canal (n)
cave (n)
coast (n)
coral reef (n)
countryside (n)
forest (n)
garden (n)
geyser (n)
green space (n)
hot spring (n)
lagoon (n)
lake (n)
mountain (n)

nature reserve (n)
ocean (n)
park (n)
river (n)
sea (n)
stream (n)
valley (n)
volcano (n)
waterfall (n)
wave (n)
wood (n)

PEOPLE

appearance
attractive (adj)
beautiful (adj)
blond (n)
curly (n)
dark (n)
dark-skinned (adj)
dyed (n)
fair (n)
fair-skinned (adj)
good-looking (adj)
hairstyle (n)
handsome (adj)
long (n)
overweight (adj)
pale (adj)
piercing (n)
pretty (adj)
red (n)
short (n)
skinny (adj)
slim (adj)
straight (n)
tall (adj)
tattoo (n)
wavy (n)
well-built (adj)
young (adj)

clothes
baggy (adj)
dress (v)
hood (n)
jacket (n)
jeans (n)
leggings (n)
long-sleeved (adj)
shorts (n)
skirt (n)
sunglasses (n)
swimsuit (n)

tight (adj)
top (n)
T-shirt (n)

describing people
aristocratic (adj)
eccentric (adj)
famous (adj)
geek (n)
sporty (adj)
successful (adj)

feelings and emotions
angry (adj)
annoyed (adj)
bored (adj)
confused (adj)
down (adj)
enthusiastic (adj)
excited (adj)
happy (adj)
interested (adj)
irritated (adj)
lonely (adj)
nervous (adj)
relaxed (adj)
sad (adj)
scared (adj)
shocked (adj)
sleepy (adj)
stressed (adj)
stressed out (adj)
surprised (adj)
terrified (adj)
tired (adj)
unemotional (adj)
upset (adj)
worried (adj)

personal qualities
adventurous (adj)
confident (adj)
easy-going (adj)
extravagant (adj)
friendly (adj)
frugal (adj)
funny (adj)
generous (adj)
hard-working (adj)
helpful (adj)
honest (adj)
impatient (adj)
kind (adj)
lazy (adj)
mean (adj)
moody (adj)

organised (adj)
outgoing (adj)
patient (adj)
professional (adj)
quiet (adj)
romantic (adj)
sensible (adj)
sensitive (adj)
sentimental (adj)
shy (adj)
sociable (adj)
talkative (adj)
tidy (adj)
unhappy (adj)
untidy (adj)
wise (adj)

SCHOOL

school life
extra classes (n)
homework (n)
revision (n)

SCIENCE AND TECHNOLOGY

computer games
expansion pack (n)
game-play (n)
gamer (n)
graphics (n)
location (n)
role-playing (adj)
simulation game (n)

technology
computer (n)
digital (adj)
gadget (n)
interactive (adj)
laptop (n)
mobile (n)
mobile phone call (n)
music download (n)
text message (n)

useful verbs
chat (v)
comment (v)
delete (v)
download (v)

keep in touch with (v)
multitask (v)
personalise (v)
post (v)
post (v)
reply (v)
socialise (v)
surf (v)
upload (v)
view (v)

using the internet
connected (adj)
cyber-bullying (n)
disconnected (adj)
homepage (n)
Net (n)
offline (adj)
online (adj)
password (n)
personal information (n)
profile (n)
real-time (adj)
safety (n)
virtual (adj)
webpage (n)
website (n)

space/universe
astronaut (n)
Earth (n)
launch (n)
Moon (n)
Moon landing (n)
orbit (n)
planet (n)
satellite (n)
solar system (n)
space junk (n)
Space Shuttle (n)
spacecraft (n)
spacewalk (n)
telescope (n)

SHOPPING AND SERVICES

goods
antique furniture (n)
ceramics (n)
designer (n)
footwear (n)

handbag (n)
jewellery (n)
leather goods (n)
scarf (n)
second-hand (adj)
textiles (n)
vintage (adj)

selling/buying
bargain (n)
change (n)
cheap (adj)
fork out (v)
half-price (adj)
large (adj)
medium (adj)
sales (n)
small (adj)
try on (v)
valuable (adj)

types of shops
bookshop (n)
charity shop (n)
clothes shop (n)
computer shop (n)
discount shop (n)
shopping centre (n)
stall (n)
street market (n)
supermarket (n)

SPORT

equipment
ball (n)
bike (n)
boot (n)
cap (n)
goggles (n)
helmet (n)
mountain bike (n)
running shoe (n)
ski (n)
water bottle (n)
wetsuit (n)

sports events
marathon (n)
Olympic (adj)
road race (n)
Tour de France (n)
transition stage (n)
triathlon (n)

types of sport
athletics (n)
basketball (n)
canoeing (n)
cycling (n)
football (n)
gymnastics (n)
jogging (n)
running (n)
swimming (n)
tai chi (n)
yoga (n)

TRAVELLING AND TOURISM

air travel
airline (n)
airport (n)
aisle seat (n)
arrival gate (n)
baggage (n)
board (v)
boarding gate (n)
case/suitcase (n)
catch (v)
check-in desk (n)
collect (v)
departure lounge (n)
duty-free shop (n)
excess baggage (adj)
information desk (n)
land (v)
pack (v)
passenger (n)
passport (n)
passport control (n)
security control (n)
souvenir shop (n)
take off (v)
terminal (n)
ticket (n)
ticket office (n)
weight limit (n)

holiday activities
beach volleyball (n)
bird-watching (n)
climbing (n)
cycling (n)
diving (n)

holiday activities
dolphin watching (n)
exploring (n)
hiking (n)
horse riding (n)
kayaking (n)
sailing (n)
sightseeing (n)
snorkelling (n)
sunbathing (n)
surfing (n)
whale watching (n)
windsurfing (n)

holidays
abroad (adv)
campsite (n)
chill out (n)
discount (n)
dive site (n)
health spa (n)
hostel (n)
hotel (n)
international student card (n)
luxury hotel (n)
palm tree (n)
paradise (n)
resort (n)
sandy beach (n)
stay (v)
uninhabited (adj)
visa (n)

means of transport
aeroplane (n)
bike (n)
boat (n)
bus (n)
canoe (n)
car (n)
helicopter (n)
horseback (n)
kayak (n)
moped (n)
motorbike (n)
ship (n)
speedboat (n)
train (n)
tram (n)
underground (n)

problems and accidents
crash (n)
delay (n)
queue (n)
uncomfortable (adj)
unreliable (adj)

WORK

jobs
flight attendant (n)
headmaster (n)
part-time job (adj)
pilot (n)
priest (n)
sailor (n)
shopkeeper (n)
soldier (n)

money
bank account (n)
earn money (v)
get money (v)
good with money (v)
make money (v)
pocket money (v)
save money (v)
spend money (v)

Exam Choice Audioscripts

Exam Choice 1, Listening, exercise 3

One
Man: Hi Sue, where are you? Can you talk now?
Sue: I'm at Jane's house.
Man: Oh, okay. Do you want to go to the cinema tomorrow night? I want to see that French film.
Sue: I'm watching a film on TV with Jane at the moment. Can I call you back?
Man: Okay. Speak to you later.

Two
Boy: Hi Bev. Do you want to come and have a pizza for lunch?
Bev: No thanks. I never eat fast food.
Boy: Pizza isn't fast food! In the Italian restaurant where I go, they make pizzas with fresh vegetables.
Bev: Really? Well, maybe I'll come with you. But I always have salad for lunch – do they make salads in your Italian restaurant?
Boy: Of course! They do great salads.

Three
Girl: Hey Joe, did you have a good holiday in New Zealand?
Joe: Yes, fantastic. Do you want to see my photos?
Girl: Yes please.
Joe: Right, let me open my laptop.
Girl: Wow, that's a great photo. It's really sunny. The mountains are beautiful.
Joe: I know. And on the right, you can see people walking up the side of a mountain.
Girl: Oh yes. They're really small. And what's that in the middle? Is it a horse?
Joe: No, it's a cyclist – lots of people go running and cycling there.

Four
Girl: Are you tired, Frank?
Frank: Yes, I am a bit. I always feel tired in the afternoon.
Girl: How many hours do you sleep?
Frank: I don't know. I go to bed about eleven o'clock but then I read, usually for an hour. I get up at 7 o'clock, so I think I sleep for about seven hours.
Girl: Me too. But I'm always tired!

Five
Mrs J: Hello
Anna: Oh, hello Mrs James. It's Anna. Can I speak to Mark please?
Mrs J: Hi Anna. Sorry, he's out. Do you want to leave a message?
Anna: Oh, yes please. I want to go swimming with him on Saturday.
Mrs J: Okay, what time do you want to go?
Anna: Some time before lunch. I can't go in the afternoon because I'm going shopping with my Mum.
Mrs J: Okay. I'll pass on the message. Can he call you later?
Anna: Yes, I'm going out but I've got my mobile with me.

Exam Choice 1, Listening, exercise 4

Claire: Hi Anna. Where are you going?
Anna: Hi Jack. I'm starting a new urban dance class this evening. I'm really looking forward to it.
Jack: That sounds great. I think Linda does urban dance.
Anna: No, she used to, but she stopped. She did gymnastics for a while, but she hurt herself. I think she's learning the piano now!
Jack: Oh well, at least the piano isn't dangerous. Are you still interested in fashion?
Anna: Yes I am. I'm hoping to do a fashion course when I've finished my exams. What about you, Jack?
Jack: I'm really into photography at the moment. You know, I think Teresa wants to do a fashion course. Do you know her?
Anna: Yes, I think so. She's very sporty.
Jack: That's right - she goes cycling every weekend.
Anna: She must be very fit!
Jack: Not as fit as her brother, Martin. He's really into free running.
Anna: Oh really!
Jack: I'd like to take some photos of free runners - it's such an exciting sport.
Claire: Well, I'm off to my dance class now. See you.
Jack: Bye. Have fun.

Exam Choice 1, Speaking, exercise 6

Anna: Hi, Mrs Smith. It's Anna. May I speak to Matt please?
Mrs Smith: Hi Anna. Sorry, but Matt's out. Do you want to leave a message?
Anna: Oh yes please. I want to go on a fun run on Saturday. It's like a race but you have to pay to take part in it. We're raising money for the school.
Mrs Smith: That's a great idea.
Anna: Anyway, it starts at ten o'clock. Can Matt phone me about it?
Mrs Smith: Okay, I'll give him the message.
Anna: Thanks Mrs Smith
Mrs Smith: Not at all.

Exam Choice 2, Listening, exercise 3

Amy: Hi Matt. Where were you yesterday evening?
Matt: I went to the cinema.
Amy: Oh what did you see?
Matt: *Percy Jackson and The Olympians.*
Amy: Was it good?
Matt: It was brilliant.
Amy: What's it about?
Matt: It's about monsters and Greek gods.
Amy: Wow. So what happens?
Matt: Well, the hero is a boy called Percy Jackson. He's half-human, half-god.
Amy: Half-human, half-god?
Matt: That's right. His mother is human, but his father is Poseidon, the god of the sea. Anyway, something terrible happens to his mother and he can't find her.
Amy: Oh no!
Matt: After that, Percy travels across America looking for his mother, but then other gods try to kill him. In the end …
Amy: No, stop. Don't tell me any more. I want to see it. Is it scary?
Matt: Yes, really scary - but it's exciting. You'll love it.

Exam Choice 2, Listening, exercise 4

Amy: I saw a great film last weekend.
Matt: At the cinema?
Amy: No, I watched it at home on DVD. It was called *500 Days of Summer.*
Matt: Oh yes, I've heard of it. It's a love story isn't it?
Amy: Yes, it's very romantic and very funny too.
Matt: What's it about?
Amy: It's about two people - the man is called Tom and the woman is called Summer.
Matt: Summer? That's an interesting name.
Amy: Yes, she's an interesting woman. Anyway, she comes to work in the office where Tom is working, and it's love at first sight - well, it is for Tom anyway.
Matt: Why is the film called *500 days of Summer?*
Amy: Well, the film shows 500 days of Tom's relationship with Summer. Sometimes it's Day 50 and then it's Day 300 and then it goes back to Day 50 again. It's different from other love stories - it's very imaginative.
Matt: Does Summer fall in love with Tom?
Amy: Not exactly - I think she loves him and they have a great time together. Tom is quite shy and very romantic - he thinks that his relationship with Summer is a fairytale romance. He's never met a woman like her before, and he wants to get married.
Matt: But she doesn't?
Amy: Well, I don't want to tell you everything.
Matt: It's okay, I never watch romantic films.
Amy: Well, Summer wants to get married, but not to Tom. In the end she gets engaged to a different man.
Matt: Oh dear. That's sad.
Amy: Yes, it's very sad.

Exam Choice 2, Speaking, exercise 5

Ned: Hi Emily! How was your holiday?
Emily: Great - Minorca is wonderful. It was really hot and we spent every day on the beach.
Ned: Wow! Lucky you!
Emily: Well, almost every day. I spent one day in hospital.
Ned: Really - Why?
Emily: Well, I was swimming in the sea when I suddenly had a pain on my foot. A jellyfish stung me!
Ned: Oh no! What did you do?
Emily: Umm, well I got out of the water. At first my foot was a bit red but I didn't think it was very serious. But then it became really swollen and I couldn't walk.
Ned: Oh no! Was anybody with you?
Emily: No, but luckily, I had my mobile phone with me so I called my parents and they came to pick me up really quickly. They took me to the hospital and we waited for a long time to see a doctor. In the end, they gave me something to put on the foot and it was fine.
Ned: Oh good. A bee stung me on the foot once and the same thing happened - it was really swollen for a few days. Anyway, did you go in the sea again after that?
Emily: Ha ha! No, I swam in the swimming pool.

Exam Choice 3, Listening, exercise 2

A

DJ Rocky: When I was at school, I was into music. In fact, music was my best subject at school - music and English. I loved English too, and I always wanted to be an English teacher. But then I got more and more interested in music and I bought CDs every week. Then I played CDs at my friends' parties and that's how I started.

B

DJ Rocky: I travel all over the world now. Last week I was in Japan, Australia and New Zealand. I play in clubs and festivals with other DJs from all over the world. It's great. I usually work for about three hours a night.

C

DJ Rocky: I love small festivals in hot places. Last year I went to Festival in the desert in Africa. I didn't play there, I just went to listen to the music. I love world music and there are some very talented and exciting bands in Africa. It was really hot there during the day, and very cold at night. It's the best festival I've been to.

D

DJ Rocky: It's a great job but it's difficult if you're married or have young children. You have to travel so much and you have to work really late. I sometimes finish at five or six o'clock in the morning. I'm single, so there's no problem, but sometimes I just want to stay at home.

E

DJ Rocky: I'm a DJ so I play dance music at work. But when I'm at home I listen to classical music and world music. I love ballet, and in my free time I sometimes go to the theatre to see opera or ballet. The last CD I downloaded was Sleeping Beauty by Tchaikovsky! I feel really relaxed when I listen to it.

Exam Choice 3, Speaking, exercise 4

Tim: I think it's really cool to be in a band.
Becky: I don't. I think it's really hard work. You have to practise and rehearse all the time. I don't think you have time for going out.
Tim: I disagree with that. When you're in a band you go out all the time. I want to start a band.
Becky: But you have to be talented to be in a band. In my opinion, you're not a talented musician.
Tim: You're right, but I can learn.
Becky: What do you want to play?
Tim: I really like the guitar but I don't know how to play it.
Becky: I do. And I've got a good singing voice too.
Tim: Really? Great - you can be in my band. What sort of music do you like?
Becky: I like lots of different kinds of music.
Tim: Me too.
Becky: But I'm not really into hip hop or rap.

Tim: Me neither. I like indie and dance music.
Becky: So when do we start rehearsing then?

Exam Choice 4, Listening, exercises 4 and 5

Martin: Hey Judy, do you want to do this quiz with me?
Judy: Sure, what's the test about?
Martin: Whales and dolphins. Do you know anything about them?
Judy: Um, a little. I went on a cruise with my parents and we saw some dolphins. I love it when they jump out of the water and you can see their flippers - they're like two little arms.
Martin: Yes, but you have to be careful because dolphins can look like sharks.
Judy: Really? But they're completely different species. Sharks are fish and dolphins are mammals.
Martin: I know, but they have similar shapes, and they both have fins on top of their bodies.
Judy: Hmm, well, I prefer dolphins! Okay, let me ask you the questions. Right, how many species of dolphin are there?
Martin: I have no idea - give me a clue.
Judy: Okay, a) forty-nine, b) seven or c) twenty-six?
Martin: Um, c - twenty-six.
Judy: That's right. There are 26 species of dolphin. Okay, next question. Which animal is the whale's closest land relative? Is it a) the hippopotamus?, b) the elephant or c) the rhino?
Martin: Hmm, hippos and rhinos are so ugly. Elephants look friendly. Is it the elephant?
Judy: No, it's a. the hippopotamus. Okay, Which whale is one of the biggest mammals on earth? Is it a) the blue whale, b) the minke whale or c) the elephant whale?
Martin: Oh, I know this. It's the blue whale.
Judy: Correct! You're doing well. Only one mistake. Are you ready to go on?
Martin: Yes.
Judy: Okay, last question. What do we call a baby dolphin. Is it a) a foal b) a puppy or c) a calf?
Martin: Oh dear. This is tricky. I'm not sure. A foal is a baby horse, a puppy is a baby dog and a calf is a baby cow. Which one is a dolphin? I think it's a calf. Yes, its c) a calf.
Judy: Well done! You know a lot about dolphins!

Exam Choice 4, Speaking, exercise 7

Girl 1: Why don't we do something one evening?
Girl 2: What?
Girl 1: I think we should go out for a pizza.
Girl 2: When?
Girl 1: What about tomorrow night.
Girl 2: Why?
Girl 1: Because we haven't had pizza for ages. Let's invite a few friends.
Girl 2: Who?
Girl 1: Amy, Sam, Emily and Josh. We can meet in town.
Girl 2: Where?
Girl 1: Near the bus station.
Girl 2: Okay, great!

Exam Choice 5, Listening, exercises 4 and 5

Female: We continue our report on holiday resorts with a visit to the south coast of England. Today we're visiting the town of Boscombe. Boscombe was once a popular holiday destination, but at the end of the twentieth century, the number of visitors went down. This was a problem for hotels, restaurants and shops, and the local government decided to find a solution to the problem. One suggestion was to build an artificial surf reef. If there were good surf waves, more people would come to Boscombe to surf. They would also spend money in hotels, restaurants and shops. So two years ago, they started work on the artificial surf reef. Today we visit Boscombe to ask 'Has it been a success?' Over to Luke Smith. Luke, what's happening in Boscombe. Is it the new surf capital of England?
Male: Good evening. Well, we're very pleased with the new surf reef. A lot of new restaurants and hotels are opening and more people are coming to Boscombe for their holidays. This summer, the number of visitors went up by 32 percent.
Female: That's great news for Boscombe. Can you tell us more about this artificial surf reef?
Male: Yes. The surf reef cost £3 million to build and was completed and opened in November 2009. It's the first artificial reef in Europe, but the fourth in the world - the other ones are in Australia, New Zealand and California. It's the size of a football pitch and it's about 225 metres from the beach.
Female: Is it a success?
Male: Yes, the waves are bigger - they're up to four metres high now. Also, we have more good surfing days. Before the reef, we got seventy-seven good surfing days. Now that has doubled to a 150 days a year of good surfing. 10,000 surfers visited Boscombe this year. This is good news because surfers spend a lot of money in hotels, restaurants and shops. People also come here to do other water sports like windsurfing, canoeing and diving.

Exam Choice 5, Speaking, exercises 6, 7 and 8

Female: Hello could you give me some information about Ireland, please?
Male: Certainly. When would you like to go?
Female: In July. I'm going with two friends, and we want to go cycling for two weeks. It's safe to cycle around Ireland, isn't it?
Male: Oh yes, it's a perfect place for cycling.
Female: The weather's okay in July, right?
Male: Well, it rains a lot in Ireland, but it's quite warm in July. I'd say the weather's wet and warm in July.
Female: Oh good. Could you tell me about places to visit in Ireland, please? There are lots of things to see, aren't there?
Male: Oh Ireland's wonderful. You'll have a fantastic time.
Female: Which towns do you recommend?

Male: Dublin is definitely worth a visit.

Female: Do you know anything about the nightlife?

Male: Oh yes. Dublin's famous for its pubs and live music. You could also visit Cork - that's a lovely town. And if you want to go to the west, Galway's very popular.

Female: Irish people are friendly, right?

Male: Very friendly, and talkative.

Female: Great. Could you give me some information about flights, please?

Male: Yes, that would be £150 each. You can fly directly to Dublin on the fourth July, returning on the nineteenth July.

Female: The nineteenth is a Sunday isn't it?

Male: That's right.

Female: Is it possible to return on the Saturday?

Male: You can, but it's more expensive.

Female: Okay, the Sunday's fine. Thanks. I'd like to book it please.

Exam Choice 6, Listening, exercise 3

1

Lily: Hello. Is that Mrs Martin?

Mrs Martin: Yes, hello Lily.

Lily: Hi. Can I speak to Josh please?

Mrs Martin: I'm sorry Lily, he's out. He went out straight after lunch.

Lily: Oh well, never mind. Um, can I ask you something? You know it's Josh's birthday soon.

Mrs Martin: Of course. It's next week.

Lily: Well, I don't know what to get him. Do you have any ideas?

Mrs Martin: Oh how about a book about photography. We're giving him a camera for his birthday.

Lily: That's a great idea. Thanks Mrs Martin.

Mrs Martin: You're welcome. Bye Lily.

2

Girl: Hello Dr Goodman.

Doctor: Good morning. Please sit down. What can I do for you?

Girl: Well, I've got very important exams at the end of the month and I'm already feeling stressed out and worried about them.

Doctor: I see. Do you usually get nervous about exams?

Girl: Not really. I'm usually quite relaxed, but I've never taken exams that are so important. I really, really want to go to university.

Doctor: Well, I think you need to learn some relaxation techniques. Meditation and breathing exercises can help a lot with exam stress. I know an excellent teacher - here's her web address.

Girl: Thank you very much.

3

Male: Hey, Maggie what are you doing in here?

Female: Oh, hi Duncan. I'm just doing some shopping for my grandmother. She needs some bread, but she doesn't like to go out after six o'clock in the evening.

Male: Oh, that's kind of you. Maggie, can I ask you a favour?

Female: Okay, ...

Male: I've started a new blog. Can you post a nice message on it?

Female: Oh ha ha. Okay - what's the address?

Male: I'll text it to you. Thanks!

Exam Choice 6, Speaking, exercises 4 and 5

Meg: Hi Alex. How was your weekend?

Alex: Okay thanks, Meg. Nothing special. How about yours? You seem to be in a very good mood.

Meg: I am! I took part in a dance competition on Saturday evening, and I won!

Alex: Did you? Congratulations. That's great news. I didn't know you could dance. What kind of dancing was it?

Meg: Latin.

Alex: Latin? You mean Salsa?

Meg: Yes salsa, and tango. That sort of thing. I was really nervous. In fact, I was terrified!

Alex: Were you? Did anybody go with you?

Meg: Yes, my whole family came. And there were some famous people there too.

Alex: Were they? Who?

Meg: Shakira was there.

Alex: Was she? Wow. Why was she there?

Meg: Well, it was a charity dance competition, and she does a lot of work for charity.

Alex: Oh, does she? Did she sing?

Meg: Yes, and then she spoke to me. It was amazing. Better than winning the competition!

Alex: What did she say?

Meg: She said my dancing was better than hers!

Alex: What did she say?

Meg: She said my dancing was better than hers!

Exam Choice and Online Skills Answer Key

Exam Choice 1

1 1 d 2 b 3 f 4 e 5 a
2 1 firework display 2 citizens 3 band 4 government 5 take place
6 venues 7 uniforms 8 locked up
3 1 b 2 a 3 c 4 a 5 b
4 1 e/g 2 b 3 h 4 f 5 c
5 1 May 2 out 3 message 4 like 5 about 6 at
6 Repeat only
7 1 b 2 a 3 b 4 c 5 c 6 b 7 a 8 c 9 b 10 a
8 2 On Saturdays my father goes to the gym or to the swimming pool. 3 My sister is very musical – she plays the guitar and the piano. 4 I love fruit and vegetables but I don't like meat. 5 My mother does the housework in the morning and then she goes to work in the afternoon. 6 My friends come to my house and we play video games or we sometimes watch a DVD. 7 I want to study English at university but my parents want me to study maths.
9 2 and 3 to 4 and 5 then 6 but 7 for 8 or

Exam Choice 2

1 b
2 1 T 2 T 3 F 4 F 5 T 6 F
3 1 T 2 F 3 F 4 T 5 F 6 T 7 T 8 F
4 2 A love story. 3 Tom and Summer 4 At the office where Tom works. 5 It's love at first sight. 6 Shy and very romantic. 7 He never watches romantic films. 8 Summer gets engaged to another man.
5 1 Wow! 2 Really? 3 suddenly 4 Oh no! 5 well 6 At first 7 But then 8 luckily 9 In the end 10 Anyway
6 1 piece of 2 never bought 3 yet 4 cool, new, black 5 in 6 get 7 back 8 been 9 was 10 at
7 1 long black boots 2 cool new laptop 3 short black t-shirt 4 fantastic new MP3 player 5 man's blue sweater 6 nice big sunglasses 7 green leather wallet 8 leather sports bag
8 a 2 b 1 c 5 d 3 e 4

Exam Choice 3

1 1 b 2 c 3 b 4 d 5 d 6 b
2 1 e 2 b 3 c 4 a 5 x 6 d
3 1 The X factor 2 A girl band. 3 She isn't into girl bands. 4 Ben prefers Shaziya. 5 Both Amy and Ben think Shaziya's a good dancer. 6 Because he has a strong voice and his lyrics are really interesting.
4 1 don't 2 think 3 disagree 4 opinion 5 right 6 do 7 too 8 neither
5 Students check answers.
6 1 b 2 b 3 d 4 d 5 c 6 b 7 a 8 c 9 c 10 a
7 1 b 2 c 3 a 4 e 5 d
8 1 but 2 Although 3 However
9 **Sample answer** I like some British bands, but I don't think they are the best in the world.
Although I haven't seen an Arctic Monkeys' concert, I have listened to their music. Their lyrics are interesting. However, I think Green Day's lyrics are better.

Exam Choice 4

1 1 d 2 f 3 a 4 h 5 c 6 g 7 b 8 e
2 1 100,000,000 2 90 to 100 3 3,500 4 80 to 130 5 14% 6 50%
3 1 T 2 F 3 F 4 T 5 F 6 F 7 T 8 T
4 1 Sharks 2 mammals 3 twenty-six 4 hippopotamus 5 the blue whale 6 calf
5 1 b 2 a 3 b 4 c 5 c 6 a 7 c
6 1 across 2 of 3 to 4 If 5 Why 6 'll 7 had 8 feel 9 taking 10 about
7 1 don't 2 What 3 should 4 When 5 about 6 Why 7 Let's 8 Who 9 can 10 Where
8 Students' own answers
9 1 First 2 Second 3 Then 4 Finally
10 a 3 b 2 c 1 d 5 e 4 1 c 2 b 3 a 4 e 5 d
11 **First**, do not pick it up immediately. It may be waiting for an adult. **Second**, pick it up carefully. You need to wear gloves if possible. **Third**, put it in a covered box with air holes. **Then**, keep it warm and quiet. **Finally**, call a rescue centre or deliver it to a centre yourself.

Exam Choice 5

1 1 on the beach and near some trees 2 sea water 3 in the sea
2 1 b 2 f 3 d 4 g 5 e 6 a
3 1 left in a place that you cannot get away from 2 job 3 chances 4 shelter from the sun 5 dangerous 6 keep something so it can be used later 7 place where you can find what you need 8 a long weapon like a stick with a sharp end 9 not cooked
4 1 c
5 1 32 percent 2 3million 3 2009 4 New Zealand 5 225 6 4 7 77 8 150 9 10,000
6 Dublin is famous for its pubs and live music.
7 1 yes 2 wet and warm 3 Cork 4 friendly 5 £150 6 4July, 19 July
8 1 b 2 a 3 b 4 a 5 b 6 b 7 b 8 a
9 1 are asked 2 I had a lot 3 going on 4 You don't (really) believe 5 was stopped by the people 6 have you 7 has been destroyed 8 weren't so heavy you wouldn't 9 goes up 10 have been taken
10 The film *The Beach* and the tsunami in 2004
11 1 It 2 there 3 they 4 that 5 they 6 one
12 1 It 2 They 3 one 4 that 5 it
13 Students' own work

Exam Choice 6

1 1 b 2 c 3 c
2 1 Because it increases the amount of oxygen in the your body so that you feel calm and relaxed but also full of energy and happy. 2 They began in Mumbai, India in 1995. 3 Julie Whitehead has been doing Laughter Yoga for 7 years. 4 Laughter Network wants to bring more laughter and happiness into people's lives. 5 Their employees are more productive and make more money for the company.
3 1 a 2 b 3 c 1 2 a 2 b 1 c 3 3 a 3 b 1 c 2 4 a 3 b 2 c 1
4 1 Okay, nothing special. 2 Meg took part in a dance competition. 3 Saturday evening. 4 She felt nervous, terrified. 5 Her whole family were there, and some famous people like Shakira. 6 When Shakira spoke to her.
5 1 Did 2 Were 3 Really? 4 Shakira? 5 does
6 1 attractive 2 personality 3 education 4 behaviour 5 sporty 6 enthusiastic 7 relationships 8 funny 9 romantic 10 argument
7 1 to 2 to 3 not as 4 as 5 so that 6 so that 7 not as 8 as 9 so that

Online Skills 1

1 a 3 b 2 c 1 d 4 e 6 f 5

Online Skills 2

2 1 It's an adventure book. 2 Suggested answers: old map, travels, dangerous people, mountains, forests

Online Skills 4

1 **Endangered animals** tiger, rhino, turtle, leopard, gorilla
Non-endangered animals alligator, bear, shark, bee, toad
3 1 Yes, there is a Home tab across the top of the page. 2 News, celebrity, travel, sports, timelines, Life store 3 Yes, there is a search box. 4 Yes, it was made in 2011 5 Reliable enough. It is made by a specialised company, not an individual.
4 1 It's from an organisation (World Wildlife Fund - WWF). 2 There is a lot of information about endangered animals, and about WWF. It is an official and reliable site. 3 There is no advertising. 4 The url ends with .org. This tells us that it is an official organisation. 5 The date for this year is at the bottom of the page, so it is up to date.

Online Skills 5

1 1 Canada 2 Kenya 3 Sweden

Online Skills 6

4 1 iTunes movie trailers 2 IMDb 3 iTunes movie trailers and IMDb 4 IMDb 5 iTunes movie trailers 6 IMDb 7 iTunes movie trailers 8 iTunes movie trailers 9 IMDb 10 IMDb

Pearson Education Limited
Edinburgh Gate
Harlow
Essex CM20 2JE
England
and Associated Companies throughout the world.

www.pearsonELT.com

First published 2012
Tenth impression 2023

ISBN: 978-1-4082-9619-6

Set in Neo Sans Std 9pt

Printed in Slovakia by Neografia

Acknowledgements

We are grateful to the following for permission to reproduce copyright material:

Extract in Module 12 about Laughter Yoga, www.laughteryoga. co.uk. Reproduced with kind permission of Julie Whitehead, Laughter Yoga Ambassador.

Screenshots

Screenshot Online Skills 1 from Amazon logo, www.amazon.co.uk. Amazon, Amazon.co.uk and the Amazon. co.uk logo are trademarks or registered trademarks of Amazon EU S.à.r.l. or its affliates; Screenshot Online Skills 2 from www.bestbooks4teens.com, copyright © Best Books 4 Teens; Screenshot Online Skills 2 for the Jacket Cover *Flip*, Wendy Lamb Books (Martyn Bedford, 2011) copyright © 2011 Wendy Lamb Books. Used by permission of Wendy Lamb Books, an imprint of Random House Children's Books, a division of Random House, Inc. For on line information about other Random House, Inc. books and authors, see the Internet website at http://www.randomhouse.com; Screenshot Online Skills 5 from Trip Advisor logo and banner, www.tripadvisor.com, copyright © 2011, TripAdvisor, LLC. All rights Reserved. Used with Permission.

Photo acknowledgements

The publisher would like to thank the following for their kind permission to reproduce their photographs:

(Key: b-bottom; c-centre; l-left; r-right; t-top)

Alamy Images: Arco Images GmbH 69r, Blend Images 104 (Zac), blickwinkel 86t, Howard Davies 115b, Chad Ehlers 8 (ctr), Forget-Gautier / Sagaphoto.com 68, Axel Hess 108, INSADCO Photography 8tr, maurice joseph 88, David Lyons 91t, nobleIMAGES 34, Helen Sessions 72, Paul Springett 05 15, Perov Stanislav 5, The Photolibrary Wales 91b, Poelzer Wolfgang 37b; **Corbis:** Alan Graf / cultura 4, Ocean 69l, 80, Nigel Pavitt / John Warburton-Lee Photography Ltd 115c, Norbert Schaefer 22; **Getty Images:** Anthony-Masterson / Botanica 104 (Andrew), Thomas Barwick / Taxi 86c, Michael Blann / Photodisc 30, Matt Cardy 050, Central Press / Hulton Archive 79, Claire R Greenway 054r, Jon Hicks / Photographer's Choice 86b, Mike Hill / Oxford Scientific 73, Bertrand Langlois / AFP 18, Ron Levine / Photographer's Choice RF 93t, Ghislain & Marie David de Lossy / Taxi 8 (cbr), Jason Merritt 95t, Cathrin Mueller / Bongarts 8tl,

Kris Timken 43, Photodisc 109, Pete Ryan 115t, Pascal Le Segretain 95b, Tim Sloan / AFP 39, Bob Thomas / Popperfoto 77t, Dougal Waters / Digital Vision 93b, Louise Wilson 113, Maarten Wouters / Taxi 8br; **Kobal Collection Ltd:** 20th Century Fox / Paramount 32, Columbia Pictures 94t, Film 4 / Celador Films / Pathe International 103br, Fox 2000 Pictures 37t; **Pearson Education Ltd:** Penguin Books Ltd: Frederick Forsyth, The Day of the Jackal, International Penguin Reader, 2008 29; **Pearson Education Ltd:** Gareth Boden 40 (Benny), 40 (JJR), 40 (Joolee), 40 (Zoe), Brand X Pictures. Alamy 104 (Sarah), Eyewire 47bl, Photodisc. C Squared Studios. Tony Gable 47tl, 47tr, 47cl, 47cr, 47br, Rob Judges 40 (Ross), Steve Shott 104 (Amy), Studio 8 104 (Tim); **Photolibrary.com:** Stockbrokerxtra Images 96; **Rex Features:** 054l, CSU Archives / Everett Collection 76t, Roger-Viollet 77b, Sipa Press 94b; **Science Photo Library Ltd:** PET / MRI 103tl; **TopFoto:** 76b

All other images © Pearson Education

Every effort has been made to trace the copyright holders and we apologise in advance for any unintentional omissions. We would be pleased to insert the appropriate acknowledgement in any subsequent edition of this publication.

Illustration acknowledgements

Illustrated by John Batten pp 12, 14, 33, 49, 61, 67, 70; Kathy Baxendale pp 15, 39, 65, 87; Bill Piggins pp 7, 85, 90; Mark Ruffle pp 3, 47, 57; Sean 087 (KJA Artists) pp 19 (top, 25, 31, 44, 58 (baseball cap, sunglasses), 74, 83, 101; Simon Tegg pp 19 (ex 2-4), 38, 58 (sun cream, clock, sun), 59

Cover images: Front: Getty Images: Mark Evans c, Werner Van Steen l; Photolibrary.com: Imagebroker RF / Arco Images / LaTerraMagica r, Mike Kemp / Tetra Images cr, P Narayan cl